CLORIS

CLORIS

Cloris Leachman

With George Englund

KENSINGTON BOOKS
http://www.kensingtonbooks.com

KENSINGTON BOOKS are published by

Kensington Publishing Corp.
119 West 40th Street
New York, NY 10018

Library of Congress Card Catalogue Number: 2008944152
ISBN-13: 978-0-7582-2964-9
ISBN-10: 0-7582-2964-x

First Hardcover Printing: April 2009
First Trade Paperback Printing: April 2010

10 9 8 7 6 5 4 3 2 1

Printed in the United States of America

*To mamma, my dearest friend whose sweet unfailing love
and delight made all this possible.*

Acknowledgments

First, to dear Kathryn Amoroso, who rooted through all the photos and interviews to round out the picture of me.

Second, my thanks to my agent, Mitchell Waters, who at all times shepherded our business with professional skill.

Last of all and most of all, the deepest gratitude to my son George Englund Jr., whose eagle eye surveyed this project from its infancy to its maturity. A grateful kiss and a proud curtsy to his patience and manly grace.

Autobiography

I had to smile. Writing your autobiography is something you do in contemplation, isn't that so? It's a look back at the traffic of your life, the places you've been, the people you've known and loved. But I can't get out of the traffic of my life today.

Recently, I won my ninth Emmy (the most ever earned by an actor), and I became a great-grandmother. In the last six months, I've made four films: *The Women*, with Annette Bening, Meg Ryan, and Bette Midler; *American Cowslip*, with Peter Falk and Val Kilmer; *New York, I Love You*, with Eli Wallach and many others; and a Hallmark Theater film. I've also traveled to New York, Rome, Cabo San Lucas, and Tempe, Arizona; had to cancel a cruise from India to Italy; been touring my one-woman show; celebrated my eighty-second birthday; and, oh yeah, been on *Dancing with the Stars*. I'll come back to that.

That's a life with some real bang and smash in it, but you know what? I like it this way; I like life to be exciting. And actually, in the middle of all that's been going on, I did begin to write my autobiography. I really wanted to get it right, and I started off determined. I picked a chair, sat in it, with a pen and a pad, and it was "move over, Shakespeare" time.

Then, like autumn leaves, thoughts began to fall on me; they touched my soul. Emotions streamed through me: hilarity, tenderness, amazement, then sadness. *It's too late,* a voice inside me said. *It's too late to collect the little girls who were you and herd them into the tale of your youth. It's too late to walk again through those febrile high school years, when you were holding three jobs and studying piano and dance all at the same time.*

It's too late to recall the roles you played; the stars, the comedians, tragedians, and vaudevillians you shared the stage with; the costume and make-up men and women you became so fond of; the playwrights and presidents you dined with. It's too late to remember the early morning when Adam, your fair firstborn, came out of you and entered the world, and the unbearable hour when Bryan, your handsome second son, left the world.

Then a different voice spoke. *It's too soon, too soon to peer into yesterday, when your eyes are so expectantly fixed on tomorrow, when your children, grandchildren, and great-grandchild are growing up around you. It's too soon to look back on your life, as if you're nearing the end of it.*

Sitting there, utterly still, tears slipped from my eyes as the times of my life gathered around me. I thought, *What's the best way to tell the story of your life? Do you begin at the beginning and follow the calendar to where you are now? Or would it be better to begin with a particular event, the day you were married or the day you won the Oscar or the day your son died, and work backward and forward from there?*

Or you could sum it all up in numbers. I was one of three daughters; I gave birth to five children; I have one

Oscar, nine Emmys, and sixty-eight other awards. I have seven grandchildren, I am eighty-two years old, I've been on six of the seven continents, and if they produce a television series on McMurdo Sound, I might soon visit Antarctica.

Enough of this inner dialogue, I thought. *I'm just going to write it. I'll start easy. I'll tell about what I've learned and what I still don't know.* Right away that brought up something big, I still don't know if there's a God. From the unkindness and slaughter in the world, it's hard to believe He's the good guy portrayed in the paintings. I tend not to believe in Him or Her. And yet, sometimes when my grandchildren and I are together—out with the dogs on a sunny afternoon or in my living room, playing the piano—such joy surrounds us, such tender emotions swell, that I feel we're not alone, that some dear, loving presence is there, too.

Right here, at the beginning, I want to say some things about myself I know to be true. I've lived my life; I haven't trotted alongside it. I've opened the doors of opportunity wherever I've seen them. I've walked into discoveries and dreams, disappointments and death. I bear the scars of not having obeyed rules made by others, and I wear the deep satisfaction of knowing I never bent to conventions I didn't believe in.

I never wanted to conform. I haven't conformed. I've tried, but I couldn't. I've never put a label on myself. I find it distasteful that people put labels on other people and say that's who they are, that one thing. When I was forty-six, people said I was in middle age. I shrugged off that designation. I didn't want to be lumped into a group.

Here's something I said in an interview with *Playgirl* magazine in 1972.

> I knew from the very beginning that I didn't belong in Iowa. When I went into town for my first piano lesson, I took a streetcar to the teacher's studio. It was the most staggering cultural shock of my life. There were all those gray people, the nine-to-fivers, sitting in a stupor. Right then I determined with every fiber in my being that I would never be ground down into a gray person. I'm not going to adopt any wholesale anything. No organized religion, no organized anything. I have never known depression. Depression means there is no way out. I have been deeply saddened, heartbroken, hysterical, exhausted. But I never felt there was no way out. I'll make a door.

Having written this much, I decided it would be wrong to write my autobiography in chapters, because I didn't live my life in chapters. The long walk I've taken wasn't divided into tidy sections. It came in arcs and rainbows, sprints and marathons, clouds and clear places.

Something else came into focus with razor sharpness, that everything I'm going to write about, every minor event, every major accomplishment, took place in the past. As I absorb that thought, I see I am in a softly lit world. My mother's voice speaks behind me . . . Music from my twenties starts over there . . . In the middle distance, a piano solo begins, Beethoven's "Für Elise." Emotions rise in me, because piano music has filled my life since I was seven years old . . . Now an odor, alien and foreign, oh yes, gunpowder, from when I took that course in marksmanship at the armory to get Daddy's attention.

There I am with Mama, carrying buckets of water from the well because we don't have enough water at home for wash day . . . Laughter erupts. There I am as Nurse Diesel in *High Anxiety*, with those conical breasts . . . and, oh, remember, there I am at nineteen, holding the trophy I won as Miss Chicago.

I could start my book with any of these memories . . . but I think I won't. I think I'll start where I didn't think I would start, at the beginning.

In April 1926, Cloris and Buck Leachman were about to have their first child. Buck was in the early stages of building his business, the Leachman Lumber Company, and there was no extra money. Nevertheless, when their first offspring was about to enter the world, they wanted to make a proud announcement. Daddy decided he'd send a telegram. That was a huge notion, because telegrams were costly. You paid by the word. Mama really didn't think they should go that far, but Daddy was heady and reckless. He went out the door like a riverboat gambler and sent a telegram announcement to his sister, who lived in another part of the state. GIRL was the entire message. That fanfare played me onto the stage of life.

Our house sat in an area called Lone Tree, three miles outside the Des Moines city limits, on Route 6, a two-lane highway. There were places for other houses, but only a few had been built, so there was a lot of space in which I could roam. We had a huge vegetable garden and some animals—a pig, sheep, ducks, and geese.

Mama had an inventive streak, sometimes we made our own soap out of bacon grease. We didn't have to. Mama just wanted to experiment. And, my younger sisters, Mary and Claiborne, and I were always wearing strange-looking dresses because Mama made them from *Vogue* patterns, and the fashions hadn't reached the Midwest yet.

Some of the ways Mama and Daddy interacted with each other sculpted the way I see the world. Memories of how they were together come back to me now with great clarity. There was never a cross word between them. Somewhere, sometime they had worked out a system of dealing with their differences. When they felt an argument was imminent, they would sit down, and Daddy would stay silent while Mama reenacted the incident, playing both their roles. She would begin by stating Daddy's position in her version of his masculine voice. Then she would recite her view in her own voice. Then she'd respond in his voice to what she'd said in her voice. Somehow things got worked out in the end. Maybe Daddy was sedated by the process.

On a lighter note, Mama and Daddy would sometimes argue about how a word was pronounced, and they had a system to handle that. They'd each put up ten dollars, and then Mama would go to the dictionary and read out loud which syllable of the word was to be emphasized. The loser paid up.

The family sat down at the same time every night for

dinner, and each of the girls had a dinnertime job. Mine was to set the table. I remember how I did it one particular night. I put a little green lettuce cup on each of our five plates, then added half a pear. I put some cottage cheese next to the pear and an English walnut on top. To finish, as Mama had taught me, I put the forks to the left and the knives and spoons to the right of the plates.

I hated to get my hands dirty in the kitchen, so I was happy to set the table, which I considered the most sanitary way to be helpful. I remember thinking that when I got married, I'd wear rubber gloves so I'd never be touched by anything. Want to know about crazy, want to know about upside-down thinking? My other job was to clean the bathroom. I thought that was a nice, tidy thing to do.

Daddy and my two sisters did the dishes after dinner, and I practiced the piano. I felt guilty about not helping, but I just couldn't put my hands in dishwater and there were plenty of wipers, and we had very little water, anyway, so, okay, Cloris will practice the piano.

In the winter we'd go from the freezing cold outside to the freezing cold inside our house. Daddy would put the coal in the furnace and get it going, and Mama would start getting dinner ready. Usually she had put something on 'pre-bake' in the morning and she heat it to the finish when we got home. If we'd all been out in the car, we'd be singing all the way home. Mama would sing with us, but Daddy didn't. Daddy didn't nurture his relationship with us, we had no kind of physical contact with him. There were no hugs or cheek kisses or pats on the back. He'd get up in the morning, shave, take a bath, put on his Mennen after-shave lotion, comb his hair, part it, and go to work in his black, four-door Buick. When he came home, he'd say hello to all of us, then sit down and read his newspaper.

Generally, I saw Daddy at the end of the day. After I'd finished my lessons, I'd take the streetcar out to the lumber company, and we'd drive home from there. It sticks in my mind that when Daddy got out of the car, one shoulder was always lower than the other. I don't think it was due to an injury. Maybe all he needed was to go to the chiropractor. I just watched him. I didn't know my father.

When I was a little girl, I didn't know anything about Mama and Daddy's courtship, but one time when Mary and Claiborne and I were up in our attic, we saw this little valise, which we hadn't noticed before. We opened it, inside there was a beautiful dark blue dress. I asked Mama about it, and she said that she got married to Daddy in that dress. Apparently, she'd been pregnant with me at the time, but I didn't learn that until years later.

I think I was twelve when I looked through that valise again. I felt something underneath the photographs and jackets and pulled it out. It was a beautiful silver tray, and on it was inscribed: NOVEMBER TWELFTH, NINETEEN HUNDRED AND TWENTY-FIVE. ON THIS DATE CLORIS WALLACE MARRIED PAUL WHITE. *Oh my god,* I thought. My mother was married to someone else before Daddy, and she never told me. *I'm not Daddy's daughter. I'm Paul White's daughter.* That was an unmanageable drama, and I was crying when I spoke to Mama about it.

"Who am I related to?" I asked. "Who do I belong to?"

Mama told me right away that I was Daddy's daughter.

She said that when she was nineteen and at Drake University, she'd gotten married to a darling guy who was president of his fraternity. They'd lived in an apartment, but then, suddenly, they'd had to move. Mama hadn't known why, but she'd thought that the problem was financial. Right after that, her new husband disappeared. And right after that, movers came and took their furniture away. Mama's father brought her home and got her a divorce.

Daddy and Mama met when she went back to Drake. Daddy began his college career there, but his father contracted what we now call Alzheimer's, so Daddy had to quit college and support the family. Right after he and Mama got married, Mama was in a very unhappy state because Grandma Leachman was totally against the marriage. She said that Buck had married a divorced woman. That was close to being a capital sin in Des Moines, Iowa, in those days, so Mama was deeply concerned and deeply hurt. But, crazily, it turned out that Grandma Leachman came to love Mama and became closer to her than anyone else in Daddy's family.

Mama was completely different from Daddy. She'd read a story to us, and her voice would be so interesting: she would become all the characters. She'd make them come alive for us. Mama always made dinnertime fun. She'd ask, "What was the worst thing that happened to you today?" Then we would all recount whatever terrible thing we could think of that had happened. Then she'd say, "What was the best thing that happened today?" It made us think. We'd all take a moment to come up with our answers.

Every day, when I came home from school, Mama would tell me something to let me know she had been thinking of me. She would advise me to do this or that. And I'd think to myself, *Oh my goodness. She's been thinking of me.* It was usually a good little idea, one that eventually helped in some way to build my career.

Mama was funny, too. She liked to tell this story about herself.

We always had a charge account at Younkers, the big department store in Des Moines. Mama went there rarely, because it meant taking the bus, and when she got there, she couldn't buy anything, because what money we did have would go back into the business. Anyway, one day she found herself there, walking through the millinery section, and she noticed a little pillbox hat with a veil on a stand, a pretty little thing.

The saleswoman said, "How are you today, Mrs. Leachman?"

"Oh, fine. Thank you."

"Isn't that a darling little hat?"

"Oh yes. It caught my eye."

"Would you like to try it on?" Noting the hesitation in Mama's face, the saleswoman added, "Oh, come on. Let's just try it."

So Mama sat down on a little stool before three mirrors, one in front and one on each side, but her head didn't come up high enough for her to get a good look. In those days you didn't handle the hats; the salesladies did. So, the saleswoman picked up the hat ever so carefully and brought it over to Mama. Then she handed Mama the little hand mirror so Mama could see the hat from all angles.

She asked Mama, "What do you think? It's certainly a pretty little hat, isn't it?"

Mama said, "Well, yes, it is a very pretty little hat, but my face is so round."

The saleswoman said, "I didn't notice that so much, Mrs. Leachman, but you don't have any neck."

Everybody loved Mama. She provided laughter and good food, and she was never judgmental and always inventive. When I was little and Mama's sister Lucia would visit, she and Mama would give me a bath and put my pajamas on and make a lip-smacking homemade noodle soup. Mama made her own noodles and hung them to dry on the towel rack. Then, when she needed them for dinner, she'd cut them up.

Another of Mama's stories goes like this: Each year a major contractor invited all the lumber dealers from different parts of the state to go hunting in Arkansas. Daddy went every year. It was the high point of his life. He'd bring home pheasant and duck and quail. Mama would have a series of dinner parties and serve these special dishes. It was a big event, she even had little wooden ducks hung on strings over the center of the table.

Even though I was a little girl in the middle of the country, I knew there were very big things ahead for me. In a way, I came from privilege, and by that I don't mean money so much. We were privileged because we spoke well. We didn't say "ain't." At school the teacher would ask me to read in front of the class. It wasn't big-time show business, but the little cues around me told me I could do things well. My behavior didn't come out of discipline, it came out of enjoyment. Everyone took an interest in me, and I enjoyed the idea of excellence.

Daddy was the trunk of our family tree. We were warm and safe because of him. We never went hungry because of Daddy's care. I don't like to keep mentioning the same point, but even now when I think about him, he's always at a distance. I guess the most accurate word to describe him is *remote*. Mama was so different. She was as close to Mary, Claiborne, and me as a mother could possibly be, always embroidering our lives.

Mama

Mama never blocked my growth with criticism. I believe I was able to succeed because of her unwavering positive behavior toward me, the surprise and delight she felt when I accomplished something. She didn't think I was the darlingest little girl who had ever lived. She just enjoyed me, she had faith in me, and she was curious about me.

Cloris Leachman, my mother, was petite, a little over five feet one, dark-haired, and pretty. Her smile had a special light, and when she shined it my way, it promised exciting things. I don't know whether it was because I was the firstborn or because there was some special genetic pairing, but from my birth, there was a unique bond between Mama and me.

She always strove to spark my creativity. When she'd present me with a new idea, we'd sit down inside or go outside, whichever the idea called for, and it would seem to me we were not only in the morning of the day but in the morning of the world.

"We're going to do some sketching," Mama said one morning. I'd never done sketching. I didn't know what the word meant, but I knew it promised something fun. Mama put together a package of paper and crayons, and we walked down our shale driveway to the two-lane highway. We turned left, and in a little while we came to an old, dead pine tree near a red barn. I'm amazed at how clearly I see that red barn right now. We put a blanket down, and Mama set out our sketching materials.

She looked around for a moment, then said, "How do you think a little bird would see that barn if it were flying over it?"

I didn't grasp what she meant, so I said, "Mama, I don't have any idea in the world what a little bird would see."

"All right," she replied. She smiled, picked up a crayon, and drew a rectangle with a line going down the middle. She showed it to me. It was a simple drawing but it brought alive the view of the barn from above. I got the idea, I took the crayons and began to sketch, and I began to experience what it would be like to be a bird flying over that barn.

One day, when I was nine years old, Mama brought home a copy of *Aesop's Fables* in one-act plays. It was the sort of thing she did, another example of her gentle way of introducing my sisters and me to the performing arts.

Daddy had a playhouse built for us by workmen from the Leachman Lumber Company. It was basically four square pieces of lumber held together with big hooks. We took our first crack at the fable "The Ant and the Grasshopper" in that playhouse. Mama made costumes for Mary and Claiborne. I already had a green tutu, which Mama had made for a dance recital I'd been in, so, of course, I played the grasshopper. A few days later, we took our little endeavor to a women's club and performed it there. It wasn't really a performance; we just got up and did it.

I didn't get the acting bug from performing as the grasshopper, nor did I then, at nine years old, have any inkling that acting was what I wanted to do when I grew up. Mainly, "The Ant and the Grasshopper" was fun to play around with.

I was first touched by the idea of being an actress when I was fourteen and in the ninth grade at Woodrow Wilson Junior High. We were given an assignment to pick out which career we would want to have. I knew for certain I would have children, that's what women did. I didn't question that fact about being a woman, and that affected the way I'd chosen a career. I couldn't be a concert pianist, because the children wouldn't let me alone long enough to do the necessary practicing. I was either going to be an architect or marry an architect, or be a social worker. And I did see myself possibly being a radio actress. With that career, I could work as much or as little as I chose and, therefore, be able to have all the time I wanted with the children.

By then I had a bit of radio experience. It appealed to me. It was fun to do. It was fun to go down to the radio station and see the people there. It was something you could earn money at, so radio actress seemed the most accessible and natural choice to me. I found a picture of an old microphone, and I put that on the cover of my report and said I'd be a radio actress.

Mama would listen to the opera every Saturday afternoon as she ironed. I listened, too, because I wanted to hear what she was hearing. Daddy listened to the variety show *The Breakfast Club*. That was how he woke us up every morning: he'd come in and turn the radio on, and *The Breakfast Club* march would play us out of our beds.

I remember only a couple of the names of the radio shows we listened to, soap opera dramas, like *Myrt and Marge*, and comedy shows, like *Amos 'n' Andy*. This was long before television came into American homes. Life was very different then. Radio was the only home entertainment, so that gave the profession glamor, too.

Movies were also a big part of my life in my younger years. I'd go as often as I could and be carried away by what I saw on the silver screen. The 1934 film *Babes in Toyland*, with Laurel and Hardy, was an exceptional theatrical experience. That film and *The Bank Dick*, a 1940 comedy with W. C. Fields brought a laughter out of me I hadn't known up to that point. The sounds coming up and over my larynx were higher in pitch and far more sustained than anything I had produced before. I learned to coordinate my popcorn consumption with what was happening on-screen: I stopped eating it when something either hilarious or very dramatic was happening.

When I became a teenager, films were even more important to me. Two out of the multitude I saw come into my mind, *Waterloo Bridge* and *Gone with the Wind*. Seeing *Water-*

loo Bridge was a deeply emotional experience. I cried through most of it, and still vivid in my mind is the last scene, with that little face peering out of the window.

When I went to see *Gone with the Wind*, I knew the picture was going to be long, so I brought a pillow. The picture *was* long. And wonderful. More than wonderful. It is what storytelling is all about. I don't know if there's ever been such a spectacular cast assembled. Clark Gable, Vivien Leigh, Olivia de Havilland, Hattie McDaniel—they're up there in the pantheon of soul shapers. In that dark theater, with my pillow held against me, I was transported to the world of Rhett Butler and Scarlett O'Hara, and they shaped my soul.

Mama never said it out loud, but I think it was her plan that her three girls would go out into the world, gain experience in the performing arts, then come back to Des Moines and create a center for the performing arts. As an early example of that plan, when I was fifteen, I earned a summer radio scholarship to Northwestern University, in Evanston, Illinois, just outside Chicago. It was intense work, because live radio acting is an art unto itself.

The radio actors stood in a semicircle around the microphone, scripts in their hands, and moved close to the microphone as their cue came up. Some radio actors shielded one ear with their free hand so they didn't hear ambient sounds as they acted out the drama. The actors had to allow sound effects to come in, anything from a door creaking to galloping hooves pounding to a doorbell ringing to a dog barking or a cat meowing. The script indicated exactly where those sounds and music would come in. They were introduced into the drama at another microphone by the special-effects man. Sometimes the sound and music cues interrupted the scene; sometimes they accompanied it. There was generally an audience, and from what I saw while I was performing on the radio, those audiences tended to get deeply involved. For some, watching a radio drama was a more intense experience than seeing a stage play.

At the end of that summer semester at Northwestern, I had earned my chops. I'd studied everything from voice production—a low register in serious moments, a higher one in comedy exchanges—to the proper distance from the microphone to tonality, to get exactly the right reading of a line. In recognition of my successful efforts, I was awarded the leading role in the final production.

Let me slip back a few years, to when I was eight. A woman named Kate Goldman was directing a play, *The Birthday of the Infanta*, for Drake University's Children's Theatre. It was a dramatization of a story by the same name by Oscar Wilde, a beautiful but terribly sad story.

Courtiers of the king of Spain are roaming the woods, and they come across a hunchbacked dwarf. They are amused by the odd little creature, and the dwarf's father sells his handicapped son to them. They bring him back to the palace for the amusement of the king's daughter, the Infanta, who's having her twelfth birthday. The day of her birthday is the only time she is allowed to play with other children, and of all the festivities provided for her on that day, she enjoys most the dwarf's performances. He dances with the same fervor he showed in the forest, and he's unaware that the children are laughing at him.

Because the Infanta has him perform for her again after dinner, the dwarf convinces himself that she loves him. He goes looking for her in the garden and inside the palace, but he finds no sign of her. In one of the palace rooms, he comes upon a hideous creature that mimicks every move he makes. It dawns on the dwarf that he's seeing his own reflection; he knows then that the Infanta does not, could not, love him. He falls down in convulsions of grief.

The Infanta and the other children come into the room and, seeing the dwarf on the floor, think what he's doing is part of his act. They laugh and applaud, but his gyrations grow more and more weak, and then he completely stops moving. The Infanta wants the dwarf to continue entertaining them, so a servant tries to rouse him. The servant discovers that the dwarf's heart has stopped. When he tells the Infanta, she is stunned, and she delivers the last line of the story: "For the future, let those who come to play with me have no hearts."

I didn't know the play, but just from the title, I wanted to play the Infanta. I didn't get the role. Mrs. Goldman chose me to play the hunchbacked dwarf. Although the dwarf is really the leading character, and the story is about him, he has only one line: "Smell the sweetness of the rose." The rest of his performance is dancing. Mrs. Goldman asked me to make up a dance, and I gave it a major try. I fell flat on my ass. That was pretty serious and pretty embarrassing for a young girl, but I burst out laughing, and that was a breakthrough. I learned something I have never forgotten about acting: It's okay to fall flat on your behind. You don't die from it.

One afternoon Mama brought home a cardboard keyboard and set it in front of me. I looked at it and right away began to push the keys. In the days that followed, I was on that thing every afternoon, and I learned to play it quickly. As I played simple songs, Mama would sing the melody. Then I would join in, singing harmony. This singing just came naturally, but it turned into something bizarre. From that time on, instead of singing melodies, I would harmonize with any song I heard. If someone, even a total stranger, was walking twenty feet in front of me and singing, I'd be behind, doing the harmony. It was just plain eccentric. I didn't learn lyrics and never sang melodies.

After dinner one night, Mama ushered Daddy, my little sisters Mary and Claiborne, and me into the living room. She said that that night she was starting the Leachman Each Week Club. I think I was the secretary, because I had a pencil and a ruler and some paper. We had a little extra money, Mama said, so the question of the day was, should we use it to join the Wakonda Country Club or to pay for piano lessons? Claiborne, my littlest sister, and I joined with Mama and voted for the piano lessons. Daddy and Mary voted for the country club. It was three to two, so our side won.

CLORIS

In a way, my creative life began at that first meeting of the Leachman Each Week Club. Right after it, I started piano lessons with Andy Williams's aunt, Cornelia Williams Hurlbut. I was first in line because I was seven, and Mary, the next eldest, was only four, too young to begin lessons. She and Claiborne both studied the piano later.

The Piano Filled My Life

When Mama delivered me to Cornelia Williams Hurlbut's studio to begin my piano studies, the only keyboard I had touched up to that point was the cardboard affair Mama had brought home. So when I came into Cornelia's studio and saw the grand piano dominating the room, I felt I was entering another world. Mama left me with Cornelia and on that first day, in that first lesson, Cornelia led me into the wonder and majesty of music.

I see Cornelia's beautiful hands flowing across the keyboard. During our lessons, I always noticed those hands, and in the open way of little girls, I always commented on them. Cornelia would smile appreciatively; she enjoyed that I noticed personal things about her. During the lessons, we talked, sometimes from the beginning of the hour to the end, about everything: school, Beethoven, the bus system in Des Moines, the weather, whatever came into our minds.

When Cornelia gave me a new piece to learn, she would employ pedagogical techniques of her own invention. First, she would have me play the last measure. I'd go over it till I knew it, and then she'd have me move to the previous measure and work on it. With that method, I'd thread my way back through the piece to the first measure, and by the time I got there, I could pretty well play the whole piece. Second, she would excerpt the difficult passages in the piece and make exercises out of them. I would practice them one by one.

At the end of the lesson, Mama would pick me up, and I'd take my new piece home. When we got to the house, I'd get out the special paper we kept in the downstairs closet and make a cover for the new music. I took great care, and when I had the cover properly fitted, I'd write the name of the piece on top. Then I'd carry it over to the new piano that Mama and Daddy had bought for me and begin to learn it.

I was eager and ambitious. I wanted to master the piano. I thought to myself, *There are only seven octaves, and each octave has only eight keys in it, plus the sharps and flats, so all in all, how difficult can it be to learn to play it?* I made the decision that nothing was too difficult. I was going to master this instrument.

By the time I was eleven, I was quite accomplished. I was able to play some important pieces, pieces that have stayed with me all through my life. Even today, even this morning, I played Chopin's *Polonaise. Rhapsody in Blue* was a special project. Cornelia said most everybody played just the main melody, but she wanted me to know all of it. Under her tutelage, I learned Gershwin's complex rhapsody from beginning to end and could play it confidently.

When our five children were a little bit older and able to learn instruments, I remembered what I'd learned from Cornelia. My husband, George, and I procured teachers for them. Adam began with the flute, then switched to the guitar. Bryan played the trombone. When he was six years old, his trombone was longer than he was, so we got him a trumpet. Then his taste evolved into what really magnetized him, the drums. He became a brilliant drummer.

When Georgie was four, I handed him a tambourine. He shook it around, and I played the piano, and we had a little two-person band. That was fun. Later, when Georgie was in seventh grade, he did poorly in music class. He was bored. Then, one day, his teacher played recordings of all the instruments in the orchestra, and when Georgie heard the oboe, he fell in love with the instrument. He came home and told us about it, so we went out and rented one for him. He played it night and day and, with the teacher we found for him, gained mastery over it.

But Bryan wouldn't let Georgie be in the band unless he played a different woodwind, the sax, so Georgie learned the sax, all three iterations of it, the baritone, the alto, and the soprano. He also plays the piccolo and the recorder. Georgie's musical talent is to me, amazing. I could be overstating the case when I say he is the finest sax player in America—I could be—but if I am, it's not by much.

Later, when the children and I had moved from the mansion in Brentwood to the lovely cottage in Mandeville

Canyon, we had separate rooms to practice in. It took me a year to complete the move to our cottage. When I was a little girl, I heard the word cottage and I loved the sound of it so much, that from then on I always wanted to live in a cottage.

I would be in the living room, playing the piano; Georgie would be in the studio, which was originally the garage; down the hall Morgan would be in his room, playing his guitar and singing; Dinah would be working on songs in her room; and Bryan would be in the living room, playing his drums. Behind every door you opened was a different kind of music. Our house was filled with music.

At Christmas we would have our annual recital, and the children and their friends would each do a performance. They'd sing or play an instrument or recite a poem or deliver a dramatic monologue. I don't play the kind of piano where everyone stands around it and sings. I play classical music, so I'd rattle off something demanding, like Rachmaninoff's *Rhapsody on a Theme of Paganini*.

All right. I'm leaving their childhoods and returning to mine. Mama was always watching my progress, not only on the piano, but in life. So it wasn't really surprising when at breakfast one Saturday morning in the early summer of my fifteenth year, she said to Daddy, "Buck, take Cloris downtown, and don't bring her back till she's got a job."

Mama could be the cuddliest, most enthusiastic playmate, but she also knew when it was time for me to move forward in my training. Daddy took me downtown, and I did what I was supposed to do, I got a job. I came home that evening a new employee of a jukebox store, where I would make labels for the records. Three weeks later, I was holding down three jobs. The second was at the radio station where later I would have my own show, and the third came out of my piano playing. I had advanced so far that Cornelia turned some of her students over to me.

One of the students was my cousin Barbara Leachman. My sisters and I hadn't ever been close to Barbara. We really hardly knew her. I found out just before I started teaching her that she had a very sad story. When she was three years old, she and her friends were playing with matches, and she caught fire and was badly burned. When she became my student, the brutal burn scars were still visible on her sad little body. She was also somewhat retarded because of the fire experience. I felt for her, and I wanted to give her special care. I was happy to be of help.

As an example of what she might eventually be able to do on the piano I played Debussy's "Clair de Lune." I talked as I progressed through the piece about how in this section the heavens were dark and black clouds were out and the moon was hidden behind them. The music was down low to portray this landscape and I played it accordingly.

Then, in the beautiful way Debussy composed the movement, the moon rises from behind the clouds, and the music swells to tell of it. So did my narration. I played "Clair de Lune" in the most emotional way I could to summon Barbara's feelings. She sat there listening, the experience of what she was hearing and feeling vivid on her face. When I finished, we were silent a moment, and then she said she had been inspired. Her words were a reward of the very best kind.

In teaching Barbara that day, I learned in a new way how affecting music can be, how it can resonate across the whole range of human emotions. Barbara and I shared a rare joining of souls that afternoon as together, we followed the moon through Debussy's nocturnal journey.

This way of thinking, of presenting basic emotions, became part of my acting. From playing the piano, I learned that the clear, truthful reporting of human behavior could stimulate laughter, sadness, fury, hope, whichever emotions the actor wanted the audience to feel.

The fire that damaged Barbara when she was three tightened its grip on her. She died when she was twenty-three from the awful burns she had suffered. She had never been able to function normally after she was burned. I don't know the precise cause of her death, but she didn't kill herself.

I have thought of Barbara often in the years since then, of the pain she endured, of her life so abruptly cut off, and always I feel blessed for the hours we spent together at the piano. Etched in my mind is the afternoon when we shared the beauty of Debussy's moon emerging from the darkness.

Cornelia was a member of the Iowa Federation of Music Clubs. When I was fifteen, she chose me to represent her at a statewide competition the federation was holding. At the time, she considered me her best student. It was an exciting assignment. I'd be playing before a large crowd. Mama invited Grandma Leachman to come, she'd represent the musical side of the family, and we all went to Ames, Iowa, where the competition was to take place. The participants did not compete against each other; rather, a jury judged them on the basis of their individual skills.

Mama suggested, and for sure she was right, that it would be wise for me to have a practice session before my performance. She found a studio just across the street from the hall where the competition was taking place, and she and I dashed over there. It was a barren rehearsal studio with a much-used piano in it. Mama took a chair by the wall, and I went to the piano bench and sat. I leaned toward the keyboard, assuming my beginning position, my fingers slightly curled and ready—and went totally blank. I couldn't remember what the first note was, what happened in the first four bars, what the melodies were, and how they transitioned from one to the other, and I had absolutely no clue as to how the piece ended.

"Cloris, begin," Mama said. "We've only got a couple of minutes."

"I know," I replied, staring at the keys, terror going up my neck and into my brain.

"Then go ahead. Play it splendidly, the way you know how."

"Mama . . . I don't remember it."

"What, darling?" asked Mama. The tone of her voice said she didn't want to believe she'd heard the words she'd just heard.

"Could you hum it, Mama? Just the first part, to get me started?"

"Hum it?" It was as if we were suddenly enveloped in a tropical disease. "I don't think it can be hummed. It starts off with that run up the keyboard and all those tricky notes . . . and now there's no more time. You haven't played a single note, and there's no more time. We have to get back to the concert hall. Come on."

Shaken, out on some far tundra, I followed Mama back across the street and into the hall. I found my place among the competitors and, still in an otherworldly state, sat down. I listened to the performances of those who went before me, and when my turn came, I stood, walked to the stage, sat at the piano, leaned forward . . . and played the piece faultlessly, without a single mistake. As I walked back up the aisle, I saw that Mama's face was filled with disbelief, laughter, and tears. I waved and gave her a look that said, "Well, wasn't that what you expected?"

I won the competition. That was the goal, but I think what was even more important to me was that I'd appeared before such a large audience and done well. That competition prepared me for the times, not too far in the future, when I'd be acting before thousands of people. The competition was valuable in another way, too. It showed me what was inside me. It solidified the idea that no matter what had gone before, when it came to the performance, I would be at my best.

A Step Into the Dark
Side of Life

When I was fifteen years old, I had done a reading for a women's group in Des Moines, and after it, Daddy put me in a cab and sent me home. It was a snowy, blizzardy night. The cabdriver and I exchanged only a few words, and he seemed a pleasant man. But when we came to my street, he didn't turn. He went right past it.

He continued driving in silence, and we were getting well away from my neighborhood. I began to feel cold and frightened, and after a few more moments, I said, "You've gone past my street, and my mother's waiting for me."

"Well, we'll get there," he said.

Pretty soon he pulled onto a dark little avenue, with no streetlights and only a couple of houses down at the far end. There was no one else around. I saw only the heavy snow falling in front of the headlights. The driver opened his door and got out, took off his hat and coat, put them on the front seat, closed that door and opened the back door, and came in and sat beside me. He went right to work, grabbing me and touching me all over. In a strident voice, a kind of voice I'd never heard before, he said, "Kiss me! Kiss me!"

I was still a young girl; I wasn't even fully developed. I had no idea what he was going to do, and I had no idea what I should do with this grown man pushing himself all over me. I was having trouble breathing. Suddenly something erupted in me, and I shouted, "You take me home right now!"

It was as if I'd hit him with a club. He stopped. Here were the two of us sitting silently side by side in the backseat, the snow falling in a hard slant outside. I was terrified. The man seemed to morph—I don't know how to describe it—to come back into himself. He opened the door, got out, walked to the front of the cab, opened the door, put on his coat and hat, got back in, and started driving me home.

When I got into our house, I fell into Mama's arms, and the emotions poured out of me. I tried to be coherent as I told her what had happened, but I was so full of disbelief and fright that everything came out jumbled. My little sisters were listening upstairs. There was high drama in our household.

Mama held me and spoke soothingly and calmed me. While I sat at the kitchen table, she made me some hot chocolate. She told me that what had happened was a terrible thing, but that what was important was that I was back home and safe. I remember being proud that I had memorized the number of the cab, 146. Mama said she would call the cab company and tell them what had happened.

The next night, when Daddy came home from work, I had to tell him about the incident. It was uncomfortable, and I didn't have the words to tell him in detail what had happened. His reaction was minimal. He didn't say much. He asked me a few questions so he could get a complete picture. I don't know for certain what he did the next day, but I heard that he didn't call the cab company. He went over there and confronted the management about what had happened. No one told me exactly what transpired, but my impression is that Mama and Daddy agreed to a settlement. They didn't want a trial, because they didn't want the matter to be made public, and they didn't want me to have to revisit that night again.

This incident got connected to a very different one eight years later, when I was in New York. On a rainy afternoon, I was in my apartment on West Fifty-eighth Street, sitting at the window, watching people dodge in and out of doorways to avoid getting wet, when the phone rang. It was my agent, Bill Liebling. He said the first thing he wanted me to do was write down the address he was about to give me. I got a pencil and took it down. He said I should go to that address the next day, at three o'clock in the afternoon, to meet Elia Kazan and to have a scene prepared to perform for him.

In those days, Kazan was the monarch of the New York theater. He had directed most of the recent stage hits and nearly all of Tennessee Williams's plays, including the Broadway production of *A Streetcar Named Desire*, starring Marlon Brando. In 1947 Kazan had forged an exclusive group whose members included the cream of young New York actors. He'd called it the Actors Studio. Liebling was very smart. I took his advice about everything, and so the next afternoon I was at the building where the Actors Studio was housed.

I had decided to do a scene I already knew, and I brought along Bob Quarry, the actor who had done it with me before. When we arrived, Kazan introduced himself. He said he'd seen me in *A Story for a Sunday Evening* and *Come Back, Little Sheba*, and he'd heard from other people how talented I was. He said we could start anytime we were ready. We stepped up onto the little stage and launched into our performance.

The scene we acted out was about a husband coming home after being away for an extended period of time. He's just come through the door, and he and his wife are in each other's presence and in each other's arms for the first time in many months. They are passionate, and they start to get into things in a sexy way. Bob and I performed it artfully.

When we finished, Kazan said that he thought what we'd done was excellent. He particularly liked the passion in me when locked in my husband's embrace, I said, "Kiss me. Kiss me." That, Kazan said, had had real emotion.

I had used what we call a "sense memory" when I delivered that line. I had brought to it everything that was in that cabdriver's voice when those words came out of him in the backseat of the cab that blizzard-filled night. This may sound odd, but I did it without reliving the fright I'd felt that night. I was an actress. I had command of my emotions, and I could select out of the past only the part I wanted, only what was useful to me.

I was welcomed into the Actors Studio, and was in the company of the best young actors in the country: James Whitmore, Julie Harris, Eli Wallach, Marlon Brando, Steve Hill, Maureen Stapleton. I learned from Kazan. He was a true man of the theater. I'll talk about him and the Actors Studio farther along. I want to pause here to talk about another man, who, though I didn't realize it then even though he was my father, perhaps laid the most crucial sculpting hand of all on me in my growing up years.

Daddy

When I was at Drake University a few years ago to receive an honorary degree, a woman approached me after the ceremony. She was smiling and had a look that said she couldn't wait to tell me something. The something was that she had bought at auction the crib I'd slept in when I was a baby. Immediately into my mind popped the story Mama had told me about how Daddy built that crib.

Before I was born, Mama would hear Daddy in the basement, where he would work long hours. He was, he finally told her, making a crib for the new baby. There was warmth in that image of a young father preparing for the birth of his first child. Once I arrived and was actually on the planet, though, I never felt that fervor from Daddy. I sought it throughout the first fifteen years of my life. I was sometimes nearly obsessed with wanting him to put his arms around me, to love me.

When my sisters and I were still little girls, Mama made a small gymnastics area for us in the living room. Basically, it was a puffy blanket, on the floor. After dinner we'd tumble on the blanket and have a rare old time. Almost always somebody would get hurt and start to cry. Then Daddy would look over his glasses at us and signal with his thumbs that we should get upstairs.

In the bathroom, we would start playing again, and often we'd take too long and forget that we were supposed to be getting ready for bed. Daddy would come and knock on the door hard, and that would scare us. When we came out of the bathroom, Daddy would be there, and often he would swat us on the butt as we went by him. It happened to me more than it did to my two sisters, and it always frightened me. I would say, "Don't hit me, Daddy!" as I ran up the stairs to get away from him. It was always a frightening experience, and I hated it.

Often when I was practicing the piano, Daddy would be in the next room, the sunroom, reading the paper after he came home from work, and Mama would be in the kitchen, preparing dinner. That was the daily routine. I tried to attract Daddy's attention through my piano playing. While I was practicing, I'd look over at him to see if he was noticing me. He wasn't, he'd be focused on his newspaper. That would spur me on. I'd play something more dramatic, more complex, something that demanded agile fingering, an arpeggio with dazzling quickness, something that demanded substantial skill.

When I'd completed it, I'd say, "Daddy, how was that?"

"Fine, girl. That's fine," he'd reply.

He wouldn't even look over at me. I had heard that Vaslav Nijinsky, the famous Russian dancer, when asked how he made such extraordinary jumps, said, "You have to leap, and when you are at the top, you have only to pause for a moment." I would keep that image in my mind when I played the arpeggio again—up the scale, pause, then down, like running water. I could not, I would not, accept that Daddy wouldn't some time notice how I was playing and be impressed by it.

Then I'd say it again. "How was that, Daddy?"

And he'd reply, with the same apparent lack of emotion, "Excellent, dear."

Pounding on a dramatic piece to draw Daddy's attention to me increased my discipline and persistence, which were vital to every performing art I later pursued, acting, singing, dancing. I was determined that the audience, whether it was one person or thousands, would watch and listen to what I was doing.

My piano playing didn't bring me closer to Daddy, so I looked for another way to gain his interest. He loved to hunt, and twice a year, during duck hunting season, he and his friends would go to Arkansas. Knowing that, when I was fifteen, I went down to the armory in Des Moines and enrolled in a marksmanship course. I went to the firing range every Saturday for the entire winter. I hated the smell of guns and gunpowder and I hated to be cold and wet, and all of those things were around me at the armory. But those were his smells, the smells that were with him when he went hunting, so I finished the course. I still remember some of what I was taught, you don't pull the trigger, you squeeze it. I never went hunting with my father. I never killed anything with a gun. I couldn't; I wouldn't. I don't remember knowing any marksmen; I was just at the armory doing my duty. At the end of the course, I graduated as a qualified marksman. It did nothing to bring me closer to Daddy.

Still bent on getting him to look my way and love me, I tried something else. He was a lumberman, and there was a statewide contest to see who among the entrants could build the best miniature house. I got the lumber together and built one and sent it in. I won first prize. That was a victory. Yes, I earned a victory in building a miniature house, but I came up empty in my efforts to bring Daddy and me closer together.

The worst thing happened one night when I was seventeen. Tommy's parents—he was my then boyfriend—were away, and Tommy asked me to spend the night with him, he didn't want to be alone. I didn't want him to be lonely, so I said I would. We weren't going to do anything intimate, and I felt it would also be an assertion of my independence. I slept on the rumble seat of his car, while he slept inside it. It ranks as the worst night of my life, because I had terrible hay fever, and between the hay fever and the mosquitoes, which were out in attack mode, I never slept a wink.

When I came home in the morning, Mama and Daddy were at breakfast. I ran past them and dashed upstairs to get dressed. I had to go to my job at the radio station. I didn't explain where I'd been or what I'd been doing. When I came home that night, I went up to my room and prepared to take a bath. I was naked in the bathroom, about to step into the bath, when Daddy came in. He'd taken his belt off, and he stood there staring at me, white with anger. Then he started beating me with the belt, not just on the buttocks, but all over my body. I screamed. I was terrified. My hysteria billowed through the house, and my sisters started screaming, too. Then my mother realized what was happening, and tortured screams came out of her. The hysteria in all four of us made Daddy stop. A frenzied look still on his face, he turned around and left the bathroom, went down to the kitchen, took a bottle of whiskey, got in his car, and drove off.

The next day I was emotionally broken. I said to Mama, "I hate him. I hate him. Why did you marry him?"

She said, "Oh, he's so proud of you."

I didn't know then, and I don't know now, what she was talking about. whatever it was, it had no meaning to me. I wanted him to be proud of me, but most of all, above everything else, I wanted him to love me. There was no aftermath. Not a word was spoken nor a look exchanged between Daddy and me about the incident.

When I was seventeen, the garden of my life came into full bloom. Cornelia turned more of her students over to me, seventeen of them. I was working for the Des Moines Register and Tribune Company, where my job was pretty nonspecific. I was to do what was needed, typing, filing, that sort of thing. There was a woman working near me who could type, it seemed to me, a hundred and fifty words a second. Watching her, I realized this wasn't going to be an area of major achievement for me.

I was getting ready to quit the *Des Moines Register* when a man from the radio station, which was two floors above us, came down to talk to me. His name was Mr. Samuels. I'd met him before, when I'd tried to get a job at the radio station, but they'd had no openings. Mr. Samuels asked if I was still interested in working for them.

Yup, uh-huh, I am. Let's go right now, were the words backing up in front of my mind. We went upstairs, and Mr. Samuels explained what I was to do—follow the ticker tape that came through the office, carrying news, advertisements and general information, and select and assemble all items relevant to women. Then, on the radio, I would read these different items. I took the job.

One piece of advice I passed on to women was that we all should empty our purses every night. It was good advice. I still follow it today. The idea was to review what you'd done that day, particularly how much you'd spent and where, to determine whether you had the right make-up, and then to sort through it all and put everything back so you'd be ready for the next day.

After dinner I'd start typing the content of the radio show for tomorrow's broadcast. And almost every night Mama would come out of her bedroom, stand there in her floor-length white nightgown, her long dark hair touching her shoulders, watching me, and saying nothing. Then she'd shake her head and go back to the bedroom.

I said the garden of my life was in full bloom when I was seventeen. Truly it was. That year I was also modeling at Younkers Department Store. Getting that job turned out to be simple. When I went to the store and asked if they needed a salesperson, the woman I was talking to looked me up and down and said, "We don't need you in sales. You're going to be a model."

My job as a model was to drift through the store, wearing Younkers' most splendid feminine apparel. Women would stop me, wanting to touch the material or ask questions. For instance, they would ask me if the jacket I was wearing was comfortable, or if I felt pretty wearing it. One time I was modeling an ensemble that featured the colors red and purple, colors you wouldn't, at least I wouldn't, normally think of combining. But the ensemble was really striking, so now when I wear red and purple together, I think about being introduced to that color combination when I was a teenager at Younkers.

I enjoyed the conversations with those women who wanted to know what I was modeling. I enjoyed their appraising looks. And, just between you and me, modeling at Younkers was the easiest job I ever had.

Another activity I created for myself made my late teen years a super busy time. Several nights a week, I'd have three dates. We were in the middle of World War II, and a lot of boys in uniforms, ones I knew in high school, were coming home on leave; they wanted to see me, so I'd bunch them into layers of three, one after the other. It was an extraordinary experience. I was fascinated to hear them describe where they'd been and what they'd had to do. Some of their experiences were agonizing; some were terrifying. One night one of the boys was wearing a belt with a swastika embossed on the metal buckle. He'd taken it off the body of a German soldier he'd killed.

Those dates were fun, and they were also educational. It was on those dates that I learned what being an American is, what being a patriot means. Those fine young men—they were really still boys—were genuine patriots.

In my senior year at Roosevelt High School in Des Moines, I was awarded the Edgar Bergen Scholarship to Northwestern University. Northwestern frequently sent scouts looking for drama school candidates to Des Moines and other Midwestern cities. The scout had seen three of my high school stage productions. That, plus my success during that summer semester as a radio student at Northwestern, earned me the honor. And an honor it was, because up to that time, Edgar Bergen was Northwestern's most famous drama school graduate. Bergen was a ventriloquist, and back in those days he and two of his dummies, Charlie McCarthy and Mortimer Snerd, were all international stars. It may be that today Edgar Bergen is best remembered nowadays as the father of Candice Bergen.

From the start at Northwestern, there was a pulse. I met Charlotte Rae and Paul Lynde, both of whom later had glorious careers, and very soon they and I virtually ran the drama department. We didn't do it by intent; we didn't take the department over in a coup d'état. The three of us were just so animated together, so full of imaginative ideas, that the rest of the drama students wanted to hang with us, be part of what we were cooking up.

In my sophomore year at Northwestern I joined a sorority, Gamma Phi Beta. I soon found I didn't want to live there. With all the girls chatting away every night, I wouldn't get anything done, so I moved to a girls' dormitory, Holgate House. There I met Jan Steinkirchner, and she became my roommate. We were a matched pair. We had the same kind of humor, and we laughed ourselves silly. Jan had long and very narrow feet. We had a rabbit in our room, and it, too, had long and narrow feet, so I would put Jan's shoes on the rabbit. It was kind of moronic, but, God, was it funny. Jan has been my lifelong friend. Not long ago, when I was trying out my one-woman show, I stayed with her in her Palm Desert home.

At Northwestern, Jan was already friends with Paul Lynde and Charlotte Rae. She introduced me to them, and from that first moment, the four of us were tied together with a mysterious brand of Velcro. Paul Lynde was naturally funny. He was as funny at Northwestern as he was later in his career. He didn't have to learn about comedy; it was native to him. Every Saturday at Holgate House, he would come and put on an opera, and we would all sing our parts. That's how we learned that Charlotte Rae had such a wonderful singing voice. Paul played the piano, and we made up arias. It was madhouse fun and another area of theatrical growth for me. I did a play with Paul at Northwestern, a Molière comedy, *The Doctor in Spite of Himself.* Molière's humor is bawdy, perfect for both of us, and I have to say we were both hilarious.

Paul worked at a branch of the Toddle House chain of restaurants, and when we, his coterie, got hungry, we'd go to Toddle House, and he'd make anything we wanted. His specialty was superb little square potatoes. He never charged us for anything, ever. Four months after Paul started working at that Toddle House, it closed. It went bankrupt. I don't know if Paul gets all the credit for that bankruptcy, but he certainly deserves part of it.

When I'd arrived at Northwestern, I had been real skinny, but I got my weight up to 120 pounds for a part I wanted to play in the most important school production of the year. I don't remember the title, but I'd read the play and had the definite impression that the leading woman, the role I sought, had to be physically imposing and well developed. When I read for the teacher who was directing the play, the first thing she said was if I wanted to be seriously considered for the part, I would have to lose weight.

I didn't argue. I didn't say, "Whatsa matta, you? You read this play. You know this signora gotta have big gonzos." Nope. I had no dinner that night. Immediately I started back down the weight scale. And I got the part. And as a result, I earned the annual faculty award for best actor of the year. Almost without exception, the award went to a senior. At that point, I was in my sophomore year.

I knew Paul was gay, but he did nothing to call attention to the fact. He didn't have a companion, I never saw him in an intimate situation with another man. I don't know if I should use the word *gay*, because we were at Northwestern long before the word *gay* supplanted the word *homosexual*. Paul was gay in every sense of what the word meant then, in those days. He was humorous, he was generous, he was imaginative. He brought lightness and laughter to any gathering; he brought happiness to his friends. We never talked about his homosexuality. I don't

44

know if it was discussed by others on campus, but it had no importance to us.

Many of my girlfriends at Northwestern were getting engaged, and the custom was you'd come to the engagement party with a five-dollar gift. I had no money, so instead of attending the engagement parties, I'd go over to the speech school and hang out with Paul. We'd improvise and do scenes. It was right around that time that I knew, without fanfare or an epiphany, that I was going to be an actress.

After we left Northwestern, Jan made sure the three of us stayed in touch. At one party we all attended later, Paul and Charlotte had both been drinking, and things turned nasty. Paul started attacking Charlotte, saying awful things about her being Jewish. He used terrible, harsh words. Charlotte got up and fled the party in tears. Jan patiently called and talked to them separately and got the rift mended.

On another occasion—this one is significant because it turned out to be near the end of Paul's life—Jan and I were at Paul's house, marveling at his relationship with his dog. The closest thing to Paul in this world was his poodle, and it was simply a joy to see the two of them together. That relationship, between Paul and the dog, was the subject of most of the evening's talk. Not long after that evening, suddenly, shockingly, Paul died. I grieved for him. I was stunned and heartbroken. We'd shared so many lively, life-giving hours together, some of the most important times of our lives. It seemed so incomprehensibly wrong that his life should end so soon.

Along with my grief about Paul's death, I couldn't stop worrying about his dog. A memory had come back to me. At a different gathering, Paul had been drinking, and he was getting very worked up. As his emotions grew darker and his voice grew louder, the dog, who had been watching Paul, walked over and put his paw on Paul's knee. Paul stopped his tirade and looked down at his poodle. They sat there, this loving look in both their eyes, the dog's paw on Paul's knee. It calmed Paul; it completely changed his mood. What I witnessed touched me to the core. I'm an animal lover—I especially love dogs—and that image of them together, the dog's paw on Paul's knee, lies in a special sepulchre in my memory.

Every once in a while during the time I was at Northwestern, a man named Bob Singer, who worked for an ad agency in Chicago, would come to the campus to hire one of us to do a photo session for one of their clients' products. I was often chosen. Without my knowing it, Singer entered me in a contest to be Miss WGN. WGN was one of the big radio stations in Chicago.

Let me go sideways for a second. It was summer, and I had a room in the attic of a private home—no air-conditioning, no fan—for seven dollars a week. Almost nobody today knows what it was like to be in the Midwest in the summer with no air-conditioning. You'd take a shower and step out dripping wet, you'd towel off and still be dripping wet. You'd put on a girdle and silk stockings, still wet, getting everything you touched or that touched you wet. Mama mia, I don't know how I lived through that.

Anyway, I didn't know I was a contestant, let alone a finalist, in the Miss WGN contest until a telegram arrived telling me so. When Bob Singer came to the house and said we had to go to the radio station that night, I laughed. The whole thing seemed unreal. I didn't wash my hair or do anything to make myself pretty; we just took off.

I sat in the studio, with a microphone in front of me, the judges were in the control booth, behind the large glass. They asked what talents I had, and I said I played the piano, sang, and danced, what would they like me to do. After a moment they said, "Would you take your hair down?" It was only pinned up, so I just pulled the pins out, and it fell in a lovely curl. It was really pretty. There was another pause, and then a voice behind the glass said, "Congratulations! You're Miss WGN." I giggled. This was the whole competition? Then I realized they were very serious, so I put on a sober look.

They gave me a lot of presents and asked me what I was going to do on Friday at the Miss Chicago contest. *Huh? Say what? Miss Chicago?* I found out this WGN contest was a preliminary to the Miss Chicago Pageant. There were twenty of these preliminaries around the city, and the twenty winners were the candidates to be Miss Chicago.

On the appointed day, I went to the theater where the Miss Chicago Pageant was being held. All the contestants were immediately given some training: we were shown how to stand, pose, and walk the figure eight. Later, when everybody went to an early dinner, I stayed behind and walked the figure eight about a hundred and fifty times. When they returned from dinner, the contest recommenced. Our walks and poses and figure eights were judged, and the roster was whittled down to three finalists. I was one of them.

"Would each of you say a little something?" one of the judges asked.

The first girl got up and was so tongue-tied, she couldn't put words in a sentence. The next girl got up, and she had a whopper of a lisp.

I got up and said, "My grandmother always told me, 'Cloris, you get out there and bring home the bacon!' "

A few moments then the voice said, "Miss Leachman, you're the winner!"

That's how I became Miss Chicago! Can you imagine! When Bob Singer took me to dinner the next night, I wore a darling suit and my crown, which I'd reshaped, with the help of fifteen baby orchids, into a little hat. The men around us were making fifty-dollar bets on whether the orchids were real or not.

As Miss Chicago, I was automatically a contestant in the Miss America Pageant. I was spinning from the way things were happening so I called my mother and said this is getting pretty serious, you'd better come. She flew first to Chicago and then on to Atlantic City with me. Today contestants have all kinds of people to assist them in the Miss America contest, but there was no one there to aid or guide us.

In the formal part of the contest, I wore the one evening gown I had from college. Right before I went out, Mama said, "Sparkle, Cloris!" She'd said it once before, when I was a little girl. In every part of the competition, I did my best to follow Mama's counsel. I sparkled.

When all the segments of the pageant were completed, I was third runner-up. That was fine with me. I didn't care about being Miss America. I much preferred winning the prize of one thousand dollars and having no further responsibilities. In all, it was a wonderful experience. My father came to Atlantic City in time to attend a lovely afternoon tea with people from all over the country. We contestants mingled with these guests, and each of us came away with a list of contacts.

The next day Daddy gave me sixty dollars to go to New York for a three-day visit. Imagine, you could stay in New York for three days and spend less than sixty dollars. It's just a tad different from today.

I said good-bye to my parents and got on the train to New York. I remember it all so well—how I looked, what I wore, and how I felt as the train pulled into Grand Central Station. When I stepped off the train, the first thing that greeted me was the heat. In August New York has some of the hottest weather anywhere. You don't know if you can get a breath.

In the station, I got out my contact list and called everyone on it. The only one who answered was Joe Russell, a publicity agent. He said, "Come on up to my office. I think I can get you a job."

In the baking heat, I walked from Grand Central Station on the East Side to Forty-sixth Street and Broadway on the West Side in my beautiful little dress, straw hat, and high heels. It was quiet as death on the streets; no one was out walking, because it was so hot. Just before I got to Joe Russell's building, I noticed an open door. It was dark inside but from the sawdust on the floor and the smell of beer, I could tell it was a saloon. There were a couple of drunks leaning on the bar and a woman standing on it, with a microphone, singing in a nonmusical voice, "I love ya soooo much, it hoits me!" This was New York.

I walked on to Joe Russell's building, which, I found out later, had been bought by a group of press agents, so each of them had an apartment there. I went in, met Joe in his office, and right away he sent me over to where a picture titled *Carnegie Hall* was being filmed. The person Joe knew hired me as an extra, and I worked for three days, at thirty dollars a day. There was an irony attached to this, my first job in New York. One of the stars of *Carnegie Hall* was William Prince. I didn't meet Mr. Prince while I was working on the set as an extra, but two and a half years later, in 1950, I was playing opposite him—and Katharine Hepburn—on Broadway, in *As You Like It*.

A few days later Joe Russell decided to go home to visit his mother, and he offered to let me stay in his apartment while he was gone. I did, for a week. He came back, and I moved to the Park Central Hotel. It was right after the war, and you could stay only five days in one particular hotel, so I was like a Plains Indian, dragging my belongings to a different hotel every five days. I remember staying at the Jefferson, where if I sat on the bed, my feet didn't touch the floor if I wasn't wearing shoes.

Joe and his buddies took care of me like I was Snow White, always making sure I had a place to stay and something to eat. I managed to get small jobs on TV shows, nothing important, but I earned enough to keep myself in New York.

Three months after I'd arrived in New York, I met Irving Hoffman, an executive with the *Hollywood Reporter*. He invited me to the opening night of a play, *Mr. Peebles and Mr. Hooker*. I have only a hazy memory of the play, but during the intermission, Irving introduced me to William Liebling, a prominent theatrical agent. Mr. Liebling and I chatted briefly, and then he said he thought I might be right for the lead in a new play, *John Loves Mary*, which was being produced on Broadway by the Theater Guild, Rodgers and Hammerstein, and Irving Berlin. They were looking for someone just like me, a sincere, average American girl type. He asked if I was interested, and when I said yes, he told me that tomorrow morning I should be at the Broadhurst Theater for the first tryouts.

I showed up promptly and was the second girl to read. The producers were in the front row. I thought I did pretty well, but hadn't done something that would cinch the part. When the next girl started to read, I sneaked up to the second balcony and watched more than twenty other girls read. I noted what I thought were their mistakes and stored what I'd learned.

Liebling and I then went to lunch at Sardi's, the "theater people" restaurant, which is right near the Broadhurst Theater. During our lunch a lady from the production came to our table and said I was wanted back for another reading. I gobbled down two more bites, and Liebling and I returned to the Broadhurst, where I read again. I felt this third reading was not as good as my first but as I was about to leave the stage, I heard a voice from the front row say, "Leachman, stick around."

I had the part.

And what I'd thought would be a three-day visit to New York turned out to be the beginning of a wonderful life there. Getting that role was not only a high moment in my life, but it was the commencement of my long relationship with Liebling and Wood. Bill Liebling and his wife, Audrey Wood, had one of the classiest agencies in the city. Liebling represented actors; Audrey represented authors, most particularly Tennessee Williams.

The funny part was that when I met Liebling, I didn't know what an agent was or did. I certainly had no idea I needed one. I was totally naive. Bill and Audrey not only handled the business part of my career, they looked out for me in other departments of life as well. Liebling represented me till I moved to California.

Rehearsals of *John Loves Mary* were not going to start for two weeks, so I took the opportunity to go home and visit the family. My first night home we went to dinner at Babe's, an upstairs restaurant that had a dance floor. That night Daddy asked me to dance. It was the first time he'd done so. It was sheer delight. I love to dance (don't miss the last chapter, which tells of my experience on *Dancing with the Stars*), and I was an excellent dancer then. Here I was at last, dancing with my father.

While we were out on the floor, he said, "I'm glad I never broke your spirit. God knows, I tried." I didn't know what he meant, and I didn't ask. We kept on dancing.

I've never been certain what he did mean, but in that moment, some part of him was revealed that I had never seen before.

Daddy died when he was fifty-two, from lung cancer. He spent his final days in the Iowa Methodist Hospital in Des Moines, where I was born. I was in the room with him, and just before he died, I said, "I love you, Daddy." He squeezed my hand and said, "I love you." That has been my treasure through all the rest of my life. Through all the rest of my life, I have carried that moment with me.

What I felt at the beginning is true. Writing your autobiography is complex. Sometimes past events seem different when you're older, different from how you've always remembered them. In the quiet of this night that is happening. I am looking at Daddy's role in my life and I see it from a different perspective. I've always seen myself as trying to get his attention, pulling at him to bring his love and affection to me.

Not till tonight has another view arisen, not till just now have I realized that I always saw things through my eyes, that it didn't occur to me that Daddy might have needed my love as much as I needed his. If I had realized that when I was younger, could I have behaved differently? What if I'd done more things like becoming a marksman, what if I'd left the piano and gone into the sunroom and sat beside him on the sofa and said, "Daddy, pass me the sports section, would you? I want to like what you like"?

That night he came into the bathroom and started beating me—I realize now he didn't know whether I'd been out all night carousing and having sex. He just saw me come in while he and Mother were having breakfast the next morning. Could it have been that he cracked because of the disgrace he felt, that he had no control over his teenage daughter's behavior? Maybe so, because in disobeying rules I am not openly defiant. My way is to be a shadow in the forest and silently cut the knots I don't like.

I don't want to absolve Daddy of the horror of that evening. He was the parent, and he shouldn't have given in to those brutal impulses. Also, I don't want to come down too hard on myself. I just feel an urge to sort through the beauty, the misunderstandings, the sadness in human relationships to see where there might be enlightenment about me and my father.

I think in my career I've looked for enlightenment. Different scenes have stirred memories of moments with my father. The relationship between Emile and Nellie in *South Pacific* has some of that redolence. Emile is older, in some ways a father figure, and when he and Nellie, in their inner dialogues, express their feelings about the other and wonder what the other is thinking about them, memories of my father and me surface.

This trip into the past has left me rueful and wondering and sad. Because in this life, I will never know the answers to those questions about Daddy and me.

Singing for My Supper

I used the thousand dollars I'd won in the Miss America contest to study voice and piano in New York. I began advanced piano work with Herman Wasserman, one of George Gershwin's teachers. Mr. Wasserman revealed wonderful things about the major composers to me. Particularly, he taught me some ingenious fingering to tackle the complicated passages in *Rhapsody in Blue*. Often when I'm alone, I sit down and play *Rhapsody in Blue*, each time with the deep satisfaction of using everything Herman taught me.

Simultaneously I began singing lessons with Helen Fouts Cahoon, Mary Martin's teacher. I stumbled upon an interesting phenomenon: all singing teachers seem to have three names. Later, in California, I studied with Lillian Rosedale Goodman. I worked with Miss Cahoon for two years, and in all that time I didn't sing one song. I don't know if she was part of some da Vinci code plot to keep me from learning words and melody, but we always concentrated on scales, breathing, and placing the voice.

Around that time I was in a downtown studio, rehearsing for a television show, when I saw a magazine somebody had left on a chair. It was open to an ad that said Rodgers and Hammerstein were looking for someone to play the lead in *South Pacific*, the part of Nellie Forbush. I thought that trying out for the part would be a good way to test my skills, so I called John Fernley, their executive stage manager, and said I'd like to audition for Mr. Rodgers and Mr. Hammerstein. John knew my work as an actress and was interested to hear I could sing.

"It's a heavy score," he said. "Do you think you're up to it vocally?"

At that moment something clicked in my memory. I recalled something my ex-husband George's mother, Mabel Albertson, a theater and television veteran, had told me. "There's an old saying in show business. Make a good bluff. Then make the bluff good." So I said, "Oh, definitely I can handle it."

"Well good, Cloris," he replied. "Learn 'A Wonderful Guy,' and when you're ready, I'll arrange for you to sing for Dick and Oscar."

There was a soft sonic boom. *Sing for Dick and Oscar?* One phone call and I was going to audition for the two men who had given the world *Oklahoma!, Carousel,* and *South Pacific,* the greatest musicals produced in America up to that time? And here's the confounding thing: the only song I knew all the way through was "Rock-a-Bye Baby." On the way home, I stopped and bought the sheet music for "A Wonderful Guy," and as soon as I was in the door, I started to learn the song. I worked on it hard for six days.

On the appointed Thursday, I took a cab to the Majestic Theatre, where *South Pacific* was playing, and entered through the stage door. When I walked onstage, I was dwarfed by the emptiness, the enormity around me. I nodded to Mr. Rodgers and Mr. Hammerstein and John Fernley who were seated in the audience. There were polite greetings then,

"Ready?" John asked.

"I'm all set," I said. I nodded to my accompanist in the pit, he turned to the keyboard and played the four-bar introduction to "A Wonderful Guy." Then, for the first time in public—the public in this case being the two demigods of the American musical theater—I sang a song all the way through.

I sang with everything in me. When I finished, there was the kind of silence you only experience in a cavernous, empty theater. The three men had a muted conversation, I stood waiting. I was so full of the whole event, I was ready to sing an encore. *Maybe they'd like to hear "Rock-a-Bye Baby."* My accompanist looked up from the pit and made a circle with his thumb and second finger. "Nailed it," he mouthed.

"Cloris," John Fernley called, "could you learn the first scene Nellie has with Emile de Becque and come back tomorrow and do it for the director Josh Logan?"

"Sure, yes, I could, I would, I can, I will," I replied. I had trouble ending the sentence. I waved to them, turned, and left the stage.

I did exactly what John asked. I went home and learned the scene between Nellie and Emile. Nellie is an army nurse, a country girl from Arkansas, and Emile is a sophisticated, wealthy Frenchman who's living on this island in the South Pacific because he's wanted in France for a crime that, he tells Nellie, he absolutely did not commit. He's invited her up to his mansion, and they're alone for the first time. The scene leads into dual soliloquies in which, in song, they express their feelings about the other and wonder what the other is thinking about them.

When I came back the next day, I had the scene memorized. This time I wasn't nervous; I was primed and ready. I read the scene with the assistant stage manager. There's a moment in the scene where Nellie is interrupted. After the interruption, her line is, "Shall I go on?"

When I said it, Josh Logan stood up and said, "No, that's enough, Cloris. We want you to play the part."

Emotions collided in my body. I was going to play the lead in the most honored musical in Broadway history.

"It'll be for four weeks on Broadway," Josh Logan said. "John will call your agent to get the business settled. Then he'll give you a rehearsal schedule. Thank you very much, Cloris. We're delighted."

"Yes, delighted," Mr. Rodgers said.

"Very well done, Cloris. Very well done," added Oscar Hammerstein.

The next day John Fernley called. "Cloris," he said, "don't tell anyone yet that you're playing the part. We have an understudy who was expecting to have the role, and we've got to handle that situation delicately. But you start rehearsals tomorrow. Ten o'clock at the theater."

Elated is too small a word for how I felt, but there was also a tincture of sadness. I couldn't help thinking about the routine disappointments in this business, how crushed the understudy would feel when she was given the news. I thought back to a few months before, when I read for the second lead in a play starring Rex Harrison's wife, Lili Palmer. I got the role, and the next day the producer called and told me they were going to use someone else because I looked too much like Lili.

My rehearsals were with the stage manager, only him and me in a rehearsal studio. He showed me the "blocking," the physical moves onstage, and then I rehearsed the songs with the accompanist. Not till the afternoon of the night I opened did I rehearse with the whole cast. Now remember, the only other time I'd sung a song all the way through was at the audition for Rodgers and Hammerstein, and here I was, about to sing the entire score of *South Pacific*. The cast knew what feelings, what confusion, and wonder I'd be experiencing, and with care and support, they guided me through the rehearsal.

I was excited. I was thrilled to be doing what I was doing, buoyant that I'd be singing a Rodgers and Hammerstein score, and performing Nellie Forbush before that large audience. I was even a little bit nervous, but I wasn't afraid. I've never had fear, not then, not anytime before or since.

That evening, when it was announced before the play started that Cloris Leachman would appear in the role of Nellie Forbush, there was a light groan of disappointment in the audience. I was nervous, but I was also determined that by the end of the show, they wouldn't be groaning. They'd be applauding.

Early in the first act, I had to hold a little cup on a saucer, a demitasse for after-dinner coffee. My hand was shaking so hard, I thought the rattling would stop traffic outside on Forty-sixth Street. But apparently, no one in the audience heard it, and after that moment I settled down. I was inside the skin of Nellie Forbush. At the end of the first act, there was long, sustained applause.

Being in a musical on Broadway is different from any other experience in life. When the conductor gives the downbeat and the orchestra plays the overture a rush goes through you, your emotions come to the surface, you have a sense of being transported. The feeling lasts throughout the whole evening. The love story of Emile and Nellie in *South Pacific* is so dramatic, so heartbreaking that at the end, every night, I was crying real tears. I can feel them pressing against my eyelids now.

After the performance on the night I opened, Dorothy Hammerstein, Oscar's wife, came to my dressing room. She stood looking at me, not saying a word. Then she lifted the lapel of her jacket to show me where her tears had fallen.

"Magnificent!" she said. And her tears started again. Mine did, too.

Later Oscar gave me a wonderful compliment. "Cloris," he said, "it's as if you were standing beside me when I wrote those words."

A Special Relationship

I n 1934 Broadway and Hollywood were dominated by the star system. Movie stars led glamorous lives and had glamorous portraits taken of themselves by the glamorous photographer George Hurrell. Stars in the New York theater signed autographs, and after their performances, they dined at Sardi's, where their caricatures hung on the walls above their booths.

There was one among those stars who stood apart, who was as much at home on Broadway as she was in the movies. She was exuberant and emotional. She could pull you down into the darkest sadness or have you imagining an impossibly romantic love affair. She was patrician; she was American royalty; she was Katharine Hepburn.

At eight years old, I was not living a glamorous life in Des Moines, and I didn't have glamorous clothes. I had one good outfit: a burgundy silk dress, with black shoes and white knee stockings. Mama brought me home from school one day and told me to put on my good outfit, because we were going to do something special.

That night she drove me in our big black Buick to the Shrine Auditorium in downtown Des Moines, which seats several thousand people. We climbed up to the second balcony, took our seats, and waited what seemed to me a very long time. Then the houselights began to dim, and the theater grew dark. After a moment the footlights came up to warm the curtain, and then the curtain rose. And then I left this world. I watched Katharine Hepburn play the starring role in *Jane Eyre*. I was awed by her star presence, by how she owned the stage. My eyes followed her when she sat, when she stood, when she gestured, when she walked across the set. I projected myself up there, onstage, with her.

This woman, who would receive twelve Oscar nominations for Best Actress and would win the trophy four times, captivated all of us in the audience that night. And no one there, not one single person, certainly not Mama or me in my burgundy dress, white knee stockings, and black shoes, could have imagined that fifteen years later I would be playing the second lead to Katharine on Broadway, in Shakespeare's *As You Like It*.

This was the crooked road that led me there.

In 1949, shortly after I arrived in New York, I was cast in a play produced by the Theater Guild called *Come Back, Little Sheba*. I played a sexy high school girl. The play was written by a young man who was already being called Broadway's next important playwright, William Inge. Bill Inge fulfilled his promise: his next play was *Picnic*, for which he was awarded a Pulitzer Prize, and after that came two more hits.

We opened out of town, at the Westport Country Playhouse in Connecticut. When the curtain came down on opening night, there was no question that *Come Back, Little Sheba* was a triumph. A buzz started about the brilliant play and the superb cast. A number of the reviews singled out Cloris Leachman as an exciting newcomer.

I was aglow. This was why you came to New York; this was why you wanted to be in the theater. You'd heard about these moments, and now you were living one. I still think no other profession can give you the buoyancy that comes when you're in a hit show. Irving Berlin told about it best in his stirring song "There's No Business Like Show Business." The Theater Guild, full of pride about its new production, took out ads in the New York newspapers that said *Come Back, Little Sheba* would open at the Booth Theater in New York on October 20.

Then things got complicated.

Katharine Hepburn heard about my performance and asked the Theater Guild if they'd let me read for the part of Celia in the 1950 production of *As You Like It*, in which she was going to star and which the Theater Guild was also producing. The president of the Theater Guild, Lawrence Langner, called Bill Liebling and told him that even though I was having such success in *Come Back, Little Sheba*, Katharine Hepburn had asked if I would read for the second lead in *As You Like It*. Langner assured Liebling that this arrangement was all right with the Theater Guild, and whether I would consider accommodating Katherine Hepburn.

As Liebling told me about it, I pictured in my mind

that night I got dressed up in my burgundy dress, and Mama and I went to see Katharine Hepburn in a performance that told me what the theater could be. It was magic. I was in a hit play—which everyone said would be the bright light of the new fall season—and three weeks before we were to open on Broadway, Katharine Hepburn was interested in having me play opposite her in a Shakespeare play.

I told Liebling to tell Mr. Langner I'd be honored to read for Miss Hepburn. Three days later I did. I entered the theater and walked out into another huge, empty space. A woman was waiting there to read with me the scenes they'd asked me to prepare. I stood beside the work light, the only light on the stage, and peered into the audience. It was dark and hard to see who, if anyone, was there. As my eyes adjusted, I saw Katharine Hepburn waving to me.

"Good afternoon, Cloris. Thank you so much for coming," she said.

"I'm happy to be here. Thanks for having me come in," I replied.

I didn't say more. What I wanted to tell her was how I'd been transfigured by her that night fifteen years ago, but I couldn't get the words together.

Katharine was alone in the audience; no one else, not the director, not the producers, was with her. She asked me to start when I was ready. I and the other woman read the scenes. When we finished, Katharine was silent for a long moment. Then she smiled and thanked me for coming and waved good-bye.

It had been pleasant, it had been simple and professional, and it was over. As I walked away from the theater, I was amazed at the oddities in life, and I smiled, knowing how much of the person who'd just read for Katharine Hepburn was an eight-year-old girl in her best burgundy party dress.

Liebling called the next morning. He had some news. Miss Hepburn had called Mr. Langner and said she wanted me to play Celia to her Rosalind. I sat silently. Liebling congratulated me and said that while this was all good news, I didn't have an easy decision to make. When we hung up, I thought for a long time about the two roads diverging in front of me. Should I continue in *Come Back, Little Sheba*, a production that promised success and glamour? Or should I share the world of the great bard with her Eminence, Katharine Hepburn?

It seemed to me like a basic conflict: sex vs Shakespeare. Liebling had already received overtures from Hollywood based on my sexy performance in *Sheba*. I thought if I went to Hollywood, I'd be a sex symbol, but I didn't see myself that way. I didn't think I could be successful as a sex symbol. I was first and foremost an actress. Also, I felt that fate was telling me something. That night years ago at the Shrine Auditorium in Des Moines, a path had been laid out. I was destined to be onstage with Katharine Hepburn. I called Liebling and told him my decision.

When rehearsals for *As You Like It* began, I saw we were going to have a magnificent production. Both the sets and costumes would be specially designed; all would be handmade and would, in every tiny detail, replicate Shakespeare's England. All of us were looking forward to seeing our costumes. The day finally came when we went to Brooks Costume Company for our fittings. The first costume I tried on was lovely beyond words. Its accents and details gave it a style I'd never seen before. The high fashion was appropriate because in the play, I was a very wealthy woman. Katharine, on the other hand, had lost her position in society and her money. In her reduced circumstances, she could not have afforded the glamorous wardrobe that had been created for me.

But when dress rehearsals began and we donned our costumes again, I noted that the elegance of mine had faded. Some of the marvelous touches had been removed. A basic theatrical truth was being revealed; no matter what the actual circumstances in the play, the leading lady does not allow the second lead to look more glamorous than she. The adage that rank has its privileges is true everywhere, but nowhere more so than in the theater.

Michael Benthall, England's premiere classical director, was our director. Also, to be sure we all spoke with perfect diction, Katharine enlisted the queen of Shakespeare roles, Constance Collier, to work with us.

Before rehearsals began, Katharine invited all the women in the cast to her town house in New York for lunch. We enjoyed a delicious meal prepared by Phyllis, Katharine's longtime assistant. After lunch Katharine said she'd like us to meet with Constance Collier. I didn't know who Constance Collier was, but I learned that she was a woman of the theater whom Katharine greatly respected. Miss Collier had started out as a chorus dancer in London in the 1890s and had gone on to become one of England's leading theatrical lights. She had distinguished herself not only as an actress but as a playwright, producer, director, and acting coach. Katharine had engaged her to be our acting coach.

We gathered in the living room and began to read the play. When Miss Collier heard something she felt wasn't quite proper, she'd stop the reading and lead the woman to a crisper, purer enunciation or phrasing. When it came to my entrance, I read the first three speeches before Miss Collier stopped me. *Oh, oh,* I thought. *Some Midwestern twang I didn't know was there has leaked through.*

"Well, you're just fine," Miss Collier said. "You don't need any help. You can go."

I was pleased but a little mystified. I didn't remember where I'd heard an English accent before. I had just reached for it and it had come. I want to say more about this aspect of my acting later on.

During the performance of *As You Like It,* there was one very tricky moment for me. My dressing room was four stories above the stage, and in it there was no intercom, so I couldn't hear what was being said onstage. In the second act, after exiting the stage, I had to fly up to my dressing room, take off my wig, my very tight dress, and everything else on me. Then I had to put on a completely new Elizabethan outfit and a completely different wig, I then had to race back downstairs in time for my entrance. Katharine was alone onstage at that point, so if I was late, it would be disastrous. Imagine the star of a Shakespeare play alone onstage, with no other actors to talk to, having to think up ad-libs.

Dick Hepburn, Katharine's brother, was the assistant stage manager. I had said to him that if ever I was not downstairs when this certain line was said it meant I hadn't heard it. So if the line went by and I wasn't in place in the wings, he should, for God's sake, run up the stairs and get me.

The dreaded moment came. First, the line preceding my standby cue was spoken. Then my cue to enter came. It was also the cue for the other actors to leave the stage. Katharine was all alone in front of a thousand people. And I was upstairs, primping in my dressing room.

When it suddenly dawned on me that I'd been away too long, a cold panic gripped my heart, I bolted from the room and down the stairs. I got to the second floor and couldn't go any farther, because the stairway was filled with people surging up to find me. They lifted me up over their heads and passed me down to stage level. There Dick Hepburn grabbed me and rushed me to the set. In the scene that would ensue between Katharine and me, I had to read two poems. I hadn't memorized the poems, at that moment, and I didn't have them in my hand. I couldn't go onstage without them.

"Where are the poems?" I shrieked in a whisper.

"Just get out there," Dick hissed. He wanted me onstage that instant, poems or no poems.

"I have to have the poems. Give me the poems," I bellowed in a whisper.

Dick threw me onto the stage, and I came to rest in front of Katharine Hepburn—who was staring at me. I do not remember what happened after that, what I said or what I did. My senses shut down. I did recognize my exit cue, and when it came, I left the stage. I circled behind the set and hovered with the other girls in the cast, waiting for Katharine to come offstage.

When she did, she came directly to me who was looking like a dog who'd piddled on the hostess's expensive carpet. Eyes burning and slowly enunciating each word, she said, "Yoou goddaaamned pig!" Then the star turned and left.

She and I never talked about the incident after that. That terrible moment was in contrast to all the rest of the time during our run. I loved Katharine and I knew she loved me, it was proved to both of us a hundred times.

When the play went on tour, I left the production. I did so with regret because it was the end of the fable, the story that had started when I was a little girl eight years old. After the last performance, Katharine and I hugged, and she kissed me. It was an emotional good-bye for both of us. The experience of sharing the stage with the special one, the majestic one—and Katharine was all that—was profound. The year I spent playing Celia was a lifetime in itself.

Sitting here amid the sights and feelings of that year, I drift easily back. It's 7:30. I leave my apartment, hail a cab, and head downtown to the theater. I enter, and there's Karl Nielsen, our stage manager, standing at his post, so erect, so authoritative. He was a navy man, an Annapolis graduate. I ascend the stairs to my dressing room. I sit at the table and have a last look at my twentieth-century self. I apply my make-up and begin to merge into Celia again. I think of my first line. Together, Katharine and I enter the plaza in front of the duke's palace and I say: "I pray thee, Rosalind, sweet my coz, be merry."

"Dear Celia," she responds, "I show more mirth than I am mistress of; and would you yet I were merrier?"

And once more we are alive in Shakespeare's comedy of love and passion and mistaken identity.

In 2003 Max Showalter called me. He was in the first play I appeared in when I came to New York, *John Loves Mary*. He was calling to invite me to visit Katharine at her home in Connecticut. She had been ill and removed from public life, and he thought it would be good for her to visit with me. I hadn't seen Katharine since our days in *As You Like It*, and I was anxious to be with her again.

We drove to her home, and on arrival, we were shown to the living room. We waited for some minutes, and then Katharine entered. She was being pushed in her wheelchair. It was a grand entrance. Even in the twilight of her life, Katharine had not lost her sense of theater.

I watched while Max chatted with her. It was a one-way conversation. Katharine didn't say anything, not one word, as Max talked and gestured. Then he looked to me to indicate that I should speak with her.

I leaned forward. "Katharine," I said, "I don't know if you remember that ghastly night during *As You Like It* when your brother Dick didn't get me onstage on time, and you were left there alone."

She didn't respond. She was looking at me, but her eyes were empty.

"I've carried that memory with me all these years, and

each time I think about it, I feel terrible all over again," I said, with a smile.

After my words nothing was said, we were in a silent space. Then four words came out of her. "What about my brother?"

Tears leapt from my eyes. To see glorious Katharine in this diminished state was unbearably sad. The sadness did not lift, for it was plain that the woman before me, one with whom I had shared that life-shaping year on Broadway, would soon leave this world.

Three weeks later Katharine died.

An Actress's Life

I 've always known how to act. In my childhood I didn't
call what I did acting. I didn't give a name to the way I
could become someone else. It wasn't a matter of intelligence; I didn't study the other person. I just could
glide into being her. While that sense, that ease, is still
there, I've developed, as one has to in this business, a way
of approaching each new role.

Here's how it goes for me. My manager calls and says
he's received an offer and he's going to send the script
over. I ask him questions. What is the story? Where does it
take place? What is my role? He answers as best he can.
Then, while I'm waiting for the script to arrive, I think
about what he's told me. I keep my thoughts loose, but I
start to imagine the landscape of the story.

I should interpose something here. For the last several
years, my son George has been my manager. He has done
his job superbly. Like a Chinese tightrope walker, he has
kept the balance between a business relationship and
mother-and-son ties. I have never been so well cared for.

We do, however, have moments of friction; sometimes he wants to give me details of something he thinks is important, and I really don't want to hear them. "Make it quick," I'll say. "You take care of it." That can frustrate him, since he knows how important the matter is and how critical it is that I understand it. While he's thinking of a way to get me to listen, he doesn't know that inside I'm smiling, because I'm remembering the day I came home from the hospital with him, and he was gurgling beside me.

Sometimes, when he feels it's absolutely crucial I hear what he's come to tell me, and as soon as he begins I sit down at the piano and start playing a Rachmaninoff concerto, and he has to find the Buddha inside himself. "Mom," he'll say, "when you were growing up, did anyone ever introduce two-syllable words to you? You know, simple concepts like *listen?*"

The piano is loud in the room as I continue working on a single four-bar phrase, playing it over and over to get the fingering right.

"Because," he goes on, his voice rising over the piano, "what I want you to *listen* to will decide what you do for the next four months of your life."

"All right." I stop playing the piano. "Do you promise I won't have to listen after that?"

"I promise." He crosses his heart.

"All right. What is it?"

"I forget."

He'll give me a brief version; then we'll go out to dinner. Oh, we have such laughs together. He has an uncanny ability to capture people's mannerisms, and we howl as he imitates someone we know. And even though I'm living the artist's life I see the executive talent he possesses and uses so expertly in my behalf. You have to forgive me for kvelling about him. *Kvelling* is a Yiddish word that describes how a mother wants the world to know what an exceptional young man her son is.

After I've read the script and agreed to do the part—and George is composed again after steering me through the deal-making process—I don't follow a formal set of rules. I continue to keep my mind loose. That's important, because it has happened more than once that my view of the character is different from that of the person who wrote the script.

Whatever the role, I think of bringing energy to it. Over and over, I've found that energy is the key to getting the audience to laugh, to sigh, to cry, so when they leave the theater, they're both fuller and emptier than when they arrived.

At the first rehearsal, I gather information. Who the other characters are and how they relate to my character tells me a lot about who I am. I begin to think about other things that will give my character an identity: her hairstyle, the books she reads, her make-up, the clothes she wears, the friends she has, anything and everything.

Sometimes, for instance, in *High Anxiety*, when I played Nurse Diesel, something external brings the character to life. Before filming began I went to the Fox studio for a fitting of my costume. When I first saw it, I was surprised at how far they'd developed it. Most noticeable were the conical breasts. The costumer and the wardrobe assistant helped me into the costume and zipped it up the back. I studied myself in the mirror and liked what I saw. I thought of a couple of adjustments that could make it even a little more eccentric.

"Excellent," I said. "What about adding some padding in the back? I think that'll make it fit better."

They gathered some padding and inserted it below my shoulders, which made the costume fit perfectly. I wanted to have a shorter neck so I'd look more middle European.

"Can you add something in the front that'll shorten my neck?" I asked.

They moved quickly, inserting more padding under the shoulders—that brought hilarious results: the breasts were lifted to right under my chin. The three of us howled, then they adjusted the padding and the breasts came back into normal latitude. Again, I studied myself in the mirror, turned this way, then that. The costume had done it. I knew who Nurse Diesel was.

On the first day of shooting, I was sitting in a chair in the make-up department, with a plate of scrambled eggs. Ben Nye, one of Hollywood's finest make-up men, applied the base, pausing when I inserted a forkful of the eggs, and then he went about putting on the mole I had asked for. It didn't stick, it dropped down and away. We looked for it everywhere, in the eggs, on the floor, but couldn't find it, so Ben put another one on. Once I had on the base and the mole, I decided I should do the rest myself. I thanked Ben, went to my dressing room, picked up a black pencil, and put on the eyebrows I thought would be right, ones that were too low and too close together to be normal human eyebrows.

As I sat there, waiting to be called to the set, I put on a very thin bright red mouth, because I wanted to look cheery. Nurse Diesel was evil, but I wanted her to have a weird cheeriness. The vivid red lipstick got stuck on my teeth, and I decided to leave it there.

Since there was still no call to the set, I tinkered some more. I penciled in a mustache. I was about to rub it off when the assistant director knocked on the door and said, "Ready for you on the set, Cloris."

When I arrived there, Mel Brooks was waiting for me. We'd never really talked about how I was going to play the role, so I said, "How do you want me to play the part?"

"How you vould like to play ze part?" he answered, stiffening his back and imitating Frau Blucher. He said a couple of my Nurse Diesel lines with Frau Blucher's German accent.

"Mel, I did that already," I said.

"Where?"

"In *Young Frankenstein*."

"All right. So how do you see it?"

"I don't want people to recognize me easily, because this character is so evil. I think I'll cover up my teeth like this so I won't be recognizable." I pinched my lips together so tightly, I could barely speak. When I did, the words came out through a tiny hole in the left corner of my mouth.

Just then the other actors arrived and we were introduced to each other. I greeted them with my unusual eyebrows and words coming out of the corner of my mouth. All laughed but nobody seemed startled. I think they expected I'd be doing something bizarre. We had one run-through, then filming began. I still hadn't erased the mustache, so I had to match it in every scene for the rest of the picture.

The characterization of Nurse Diesel, then, was borne not through my making a deep analysis of her character or a study of her family background, but from the imagination of the costume designer. This illustrates that for me the source of a performance might be almost anything, could come from almost anywhere. It starts with staying loose and opening the doors to ideas and imagination.

I don't have a whole catechism on acting but I would say these things are essential parts of my foundation.

> A. Acting is make-believe. Don't make it a problem. It's spontaneous. Have fun.
> B. Audiences aren't judgmental; they're your friends.
> C. The lines of a play are just clues, something to build on.
> D. Don't be afraid you're going to make a fool of yourself.

Other Thoughts About Acting

E very once in a while I realize how different acting is from most other people's areas of life. Last month I talked to a group of businesswomen, that was really different because show business is in a different world than business business. Even the word *business* means different things. On stage, business is something you do during a scene . . . pour champagne, straighten the pillows on the sofa, dust the table, do your nails while you're talking on the phone.

In business business, you go to school and get an MBA or become a CPA or an MP3. You learn to generate income, diversify your stock portfolio, grow your assets. Deciding to be in show business isn't anything like that. It's not an exercise in logic; it's not something you discuss with career counselors. It's a blood disease with no known cure, and it's a lifelong mental spasm.

Most actors don't know about business, so they have business managers. I have a business manager. I see him occasionally at parties. I wave to him, but I avoid being alone with him because if he gets me in his office, he wants to talk about, uh-huh, business. I have trouble concentrating when he talks. He says the words *estate planning* and immediately I see myself in a horse-drawn carriage riding up to a magnificent Southern mansion. Rhett Butler is there with a landscape architect, a flower expert, and a soil specialist, and—"Great balls of fire, Melanie. We're going to do some estate plannin'."

There's another big difference between show business and business business, the rewards. You can earn a lot of money in show business, but that's not why you're there. That's not why I've been in show business all my life. I can see all the things I'd have missed if I'd gone into dentistry or sold Tupperware or owned a delicatessen—I once pictured myself greeting customers in my deli. "Yes, sir, madam, what'll it be, please? Today we got corned beef so good, it falls off your fork, pastrami that glows in the dark, tongue that melts on your—tongue. Which beautiful thing you wanna take home?"

If I'd chosen a different career, I wouldn't have been to the White House, wouldn't have gone to the Academy Awards, wouldn't have lived four houses away from Judy Garland, and had her daughter Lorna Luft in our house so often, she was like one of my own.

Lorna is the daughter of Judy Garland and Sid Luft, to whom Judy had previously been married. Lorna came over to our house all the time with other neighborhood kids, particularly with her friend Katey Sagal. Katey also grew up with our kids, and she was especially close to Bryan. She became a highly successful actress. She starred in the TV series *Married with Children*. At the funeral ceremony we had for Bryan, Katie sang "Amazing Grace" alone, with no accompaniment.

I made the linen closet, at the top of the stairs in our house, to be what I called the Screaming Room. If you need to scream, you just open the door and go in there and bellow. The girls loved it. It became a little playroom, they'd go in there and talk for hours.

Lorna and Katey came over one day wearing serious expressions. They sat me down in the breakfast room and pulled up their chairs opposite me. They didn't hesitate. They didn't skirt around the subject. They came right out and said that they wanted me to adopt them. It took a while to digest what they'd said and to consider what about their lives had given birth to this idea.

We began a very real talk, and they told me more of the details of their lives. Basically, they felt they had no family, no stability. Our house, and the way our boys were growing up, was a picture to them of how family life could be, they wanted their lives to be like those of our boys. I felt I had to proceed slowly. This was delicate. They meant what they said, and I could not give an offhand answer.

First, I assured them they could come over and see me anytime, day or night. It didn't matter. I would always be ready to talk with them. About the idea of me adopting them, I told them that we would be wise to take it slowly. We would not rule it out, but work on improving their home situations first.

One evening, not long after my meeting with the girls, I got a call from the neighbors up the street, near Sunset

Boulevard. I'd actually never met them, but they said both Judy's children, Lorna and Joey, were with them, and could I go and take care of Judy. She was alone in the house, and the children were very worried that she might drown herself.

I turned off everything in the kitchen, tore out of my house, and raced up to Judy's. She was in the swimming pool, listless, not moving, and I pulled her out. We went into her house. She was deeply depressed, terribly upset. I wanted to get her to talk about what had brought her to this state. We did talk, till three in the morning. Along the way she offered me some chicken soup she'd made. It was dear and sweet to share it with her.

The saddest moment came when she dissolved into tears—I mean a deluge—and said, "Why can't any man love me?" I put my arms around her and held her. I kept the conversation going until her emotions settled down, I stayed till she made her way to bed. Then I went home.

The next time I saw Judy was at a party at Pat and Peter Lawford's house. Pat was President Kennedy's sister; Peter was a movie star, and very close to the president. It was a festive party. Bobby Kennedy and Ted Kennedy were there, Gene Kelly and Marilyn Monroe. Marilyn and Bobby Kennedy were in the living room, dancing in a very sexy way. Many of the guests were around the edges of the room, pretending not to notice, and, of course, trying to hear every whisper that passed between them. Marilyn and Bobby took no notice.

When you met Marilyn she was even more gorgeous, more voluptuous—her eyes, her mouth, her body—in person than she appeared in her pictures. But I saw her as part of a classic Hollywood pattern: a beautiful young girl comes to town, her exquisite face and body wow the industry, and she becomes a star. But inside, she's still the ordinary person she's been since she grew up. She's had no training in being a star, has no knowledge of how to meet the assaults and pressures that come with this new status.

Marilyn was not just a star. She was a supernova, so when she got into her thirties and her body started to lose its tension, her face to take on wrinkles, who was she to herself but that small-town girl who was worshipped for magnificent physical qualities that were now ebbing away.

My impression of Bobby Kennedy was that he had far less of the humor, the savoir faire, that characterized Jack and Teddy. To me, he seemed cold in comparison to his brothers. I remember hearing a story about Bobby that corroborates this impression. As the 1960 Democratic National Convention, held in Los Angeles, was nearing its end, the race for the nomination was very close. The night before the vote Bobby, who was Jack's campaign manager, went to the caucus rooms of the major delegations and said to each of them, "We're going to win, and if you vote against us, we won't forget it."

Seeing them all at Pat and Peter Lawford's party was sort of sad for me. We all knew that Marilyn had been having an affair with the president; she'd sung that sexy version of "Happy Birthday" to him at his party at the White House earlier that year. Now it seemed that Jack was done with her and had passed her on to Bobby. When, not long after, Marilyn died, I wondered if I'd guessed right, that she'd been heartbroken at being sent down the line of Kennedy brothers.

Judy and I chatted cordially at that party, and neither of us mentioned or referred to the emotional night of a couple of weeks earlier. That was fine with me; I was glad to see her alive and stable and in a party mood. Her daughter Liza had visited her, and I think that made her feel better, too.

Near the end of the evening, Ted Kennedy and his roommate from law school, John Tunney, the son of Gene Tunney, the famous boxer who defeated Jack Dempsey twice, stood up and took over the room. John, who would be elected to the U.S. Senate in 1970, and Ted put on a little show. They set what looked like a soapbox in the center of the room. John stepped up on it, and Ted fired political questions at him, one after the other. John's answers came back just as fast and with real intelligence. Then Ted got on the box, and they repeated the exercise. I must say it was impressive. The questions were intelligent, and the answers were spot-on. I don't know how our major politicians today would fare under such an interrogative assault.

To continue about my chosen career, if I hadn't been an actress, I would never have met my husband, George Englund. His sister Patsy was in the 1950 Broadway production of *As You Like It*, the one in which I played Celia. One night George came backstage, and the car I was driving suddenly changed lanes. Not too long after, we were married, we had five children and we've sailed most of the ocean of life in the same bobbing craft we started with. We got divorced along the way, but we're still together in all the important ways. George will appear in fuller detail later on.

Another thing about the business of acting—because acting today *is* a business and like every other business, it's been changed by technology. When I began acting, you learned to perform on the stage, to develop a character from the inside. Then, if fortune smiled, you'd begin acting in films and you'd learn film technique.

Today it's become much more specialized, sub-divided. These days there are actors who do only commercials. In those you don't develop a character; you go from zero to sixty in a split second. On cue you have to squeal, "Wow! That yogurt is a blast! I want MORE!"

Soap operas are another specialized field. There are usually twelve or more stories going on at the same time in a soap opera, so the actors are always having to remind the audience which story they're in. To do it they tell each other about what happened the last time they were involved in this story. You hear things like: "Are you saying, Bosley, that Tim told Tina that when Madge arrives from Yonkers with her Dalmatians, she's going to learn that David Dermont's sister is suffering from acromegaly and has a forehead only three quarters of an inch high?"

My son Morgan was on the soap opera *Guiding Light* for a long period. He'd been around actors and acting all his life but didn't really consider acting as something for him to do until he got to New York. Someone brought him to the Circle in the Square Theatre, and he liked what he saw and decided to try acting. He began studying at the Circle, and not long after he started, he was selected to play in a production of *Picnic*.

His experience in New York was so different from mine. He had to start out in a small apartment, get his photograph composite together, make rounds, call on casting directors, the usual pattern for an actor starting out.

For me, it had been just the opposite. I never had a cold-water flat or made rounds or dropped off pictures. I never had any pictures. I would be in a play or a television show, and a producer or director would see me in it and ask me to be in his play or television show. After I left the Actors Studio, reality set in. I didn't work for a year, that's when I began to realize there was competition out there.

When Morgan decided to be an actor, I was happy he'd found something he liked and that really interested him. He'd been studying for only four or five months, I think, when he got the part of Dylan on *Guiding Light*. He was on it for six years, from 1989 to 1995.

When Morgan got married, he had a little girl, and two years later, a little boy, and it was getting difficult to live in New York. Also, he'd determined by then he didn't want to be a soap actor. He wanted to be on the stage, on television, and in films. He came back to California and, in effect, started a new career. There were problems: He didn't have representation out here, that was one handicap. He'd go on a call to read for a part, and a thousand sexy blond studs would also be there. Also, he'd get the chance to read for a part, and half the time he'd have to take the kids with him.

He realized this life wasn't for him. He liked acting, but being an actor, living the life of an actor with all its uncertainty and instability, no, there would be something more fulfilling. He found that something else. He went back to school and became a certified paramedic. Then he decided to become a firefighter. And now Morgan Englund is a full-fledged paramedic fireman, happy that the work he is doing has immediate effect on people's lives. Often his knowledge, his ability to act swiftly is the difference between whether the person he is attending lives or dies.

Every day his life is filled with dramatic events, some tragic, some comical. On one call he was attending to a woman suffering from severe heat and smoke inhalation. She was an emotional wreck. He had put her on a gurney, and as he bent over her, talking soothingly and applying the oxygen mask to her, she whipped off the mask, sat upright, and screamed, "Dylan!" She was a soap opera addict and absolutely could not believe that one of the characters she loved best was there helping to save her life.

Speaking of different stories going on at the same time, I want to pick up the tale of when I arrived in New York. I'd come back to the Big Apple after my visit home and immediately started rehearsals of *John Loves Mary*. On the third day, just before we were to take our places, Josh Logan, the director, called me over to where he was. I went. He looked very upset. In fact, there were tears in his eyes.

"Cloris," he said, "I don't know how to say this, but we've got to replace you. When Norman Krasna, the author of the play, heard we'd hired a Miss America contestant to play Mary, he said he didn't believe such a person could possibly portray the sophisticated daughter of a United States senator. He has cast approval, and he wants an actress named Nina Foch to play the part. In fact, he's brought her with him to New York."

I told Josh I understood and that I was all right with it. He said he was grateful I'd taken it so calmly. In fact, I was calm. I wasn't bothered at all. I thought, *There'll be another streetcar coming along.* That was an unexpected event, the first big issue in my career, but it was true that I wasn't upset and that attitude of giving no big emotion to the bumps when they come has been a consistent theme through my life. Here's a quote from a *New York Times* interview I did in 1959.

"I've never taken acting seriously. I just can't feel it's a matter of life or death whether I get a part or not . . . I won't fight for a role, I wait for it to come to me."

They asked me to understudy Nina Foch as well as another role in *John Loves Mary*, and I agreed. At the same time, I was understudying five separate roles in the play *Happy Birthday*, including the lead role, which was being performed by the first lady of the American theater, Helen Hayes.

From watching her performance, I didn't understand why Helen Hayes was given that accolade. I thought she was nice but not wonderful, not thrilling. Since the play had been written for her, it occurred to me that that could be the reason she seemed less than glowing. She simply wasn't being challenged. Watching her gave me confidence in myself.

I checked in at all performances of *John Loves Mary* at the Music Box Theater, then I would go through Schubert Alley to the Plymouth Theater and check in there. Then I'd go back to the Music Box basement and sit with the other understudies.

At different times I played both roles in *John Loves Mary* and all five roles in *Happy Birthday*. I was always ready to go on in any of the roles. I never had any fear. One night, when I was playing one of the characters in *Happy Birthday*, Ms. Hayes leaned over to me in the middle of the performance and asked me how in the world I did it. I said, "Guts. That's all." Afterward, I worried that saying "guts" to the first lady of the American theater might have seemed a little cheeky.

It finally dawned on the producers of both shows that there was a considerable logistical problem in my covering roles in both productions. What if I was needed in both theaters at the same time? The solution was to hire an understudy for me, so that added one more chair to the nightly convention of understudies in the basement of the Music Box Theater.

Daytimes were getting increasingly busy. I was working almost nonstop on television shows while understudying those seven roles at night. I was never tired, never fearful, never overwhelmed. I was enjoying every minute of my life. There were three of us who got most of the good roles: Maria Riva, Marlene Dietrich's daughter; Anne Marno, who would later become Anne Bancroft; and myself. The big television shows then were *Studio One, The Ford Theater, The*

Philco Television Playhouse, and *Lights Out.* I wish I could remember every single one of them.

It was called the Golden Age of Television, and truly, it was that. Television was a brand-new medium, and it called for new talent, new ideas, and innovation. America was lucky; that era was studded with young talented writers, directors, and actors. Paddy Chayefsky, for instance, wrote the teleplay *Marty*, which, when made into a movie, gave Ernest Borgnine his first starring role and kicked off his long, illustrious career. In my opinion, among all his shining performances, Marty is still Ernie's best one. He was memorable. A number of other television dramas that were produced then were subsequently made into films.

It was the Golden Age of Television, and it was *live* television. I stress that word because acting went through a metamorphosis: your performance and everything else in a television show had to be fitted into exactly one hour. That meant a number of new demands on the actor. A one-hour show became a combination of acting; sprinting to the next set; changing make-up, if you had to have scars added, for instance; and never showing the tension, never getting out of character.

The large cameras were on rollers and were pushed around by the camera operator, who would occasionally have to hold you in close-up as his camera followed you to the next set. Sometimes you would be leaning against a lamppost, doing a soliloquy in close-up, while you and the costumer were changing your whole outfit. So you had to be concentrating in a new way, doing a high-technology dance with the camera, and trying to remember your lines while others were undressing you.

The assistant director would stand by the camera and give directions as needed. If we were running behind, he would give the "pick it up" sign, revolving his hand, with his index finger extended. If the show was going too quickly, he would put his two hands in front of him and slowly separate them, as if he were pulling taffy, which meant slow down. He would be getting instructions from the control booth and passing them on to us in this somewhat primitive way.

The system caused odd things to happen. One time, as we neared the end of a show, the name of which I don't remember, Steve Hill, a fine actor and a member of the Actors Studio, who later had a starring role on *Law & Order*, had the wrap-up monologue. In it he revealed the whole mystery of the drama. He started into it when the assistant director dramatically gave him the taffy pull, slow it down. Steve slowed his speech, and the assistant director gave him the taffy pull again. Steve slowed down even more, and again, he was given the "slow it down" signal. Finally, it got to the point where he couldn't remember his words, because he had to space them so far apart. To us on the set, the experience was totally bizarre. It was as if Steve had just won the Slow Talkers of America Championship.

I remember three incidents with elderly actors on the set of a telelvision show. In one incident the actor completely forgot his lines. He stammered and stuttered, and none of us knew how to help him. Suddenly his lines were shouted over the loudspeaker from the control booth;

they had shut off the live sound long enough to holler his words to him. He picked them up and went blithely on.

Another incident occurred during the filming of a courtroom drama. The man playing the judge had been shaky throughout the whole show, standing on his podium, he said to the three of us in front of him, "I've decided to let you go free." He turned away and stepped off the podium. He could tell by the shock on our faces that what he'd said was completely wrong, so, totally unraveled, he stepped back up on the podium and said in a stronger voice, with a tinge of hysteria in it, "I've changed my mind. The three of you are going to jail!"

That wasn't the right line, either. He was supposed to say, "I've heard enough. This case is going to trial." The three of us thought up some ad-libs, and Bob Quarry, one of the actors, helped the older man off the set; he virtually had to carry him.

It must have been that the tension of live television built up during the show, because in the crucial moments at the end was when the elderly actors seemed to lose it. The last incident I want to describe was where we, the family, were gathered at the bottom of the stairs in our elegant house to hear our aged uncle tell us what he was going to do with his fortune, that is, how much would be left to each of us. As he slowly descended the stairs, he had a look of semi-beatitude on his face. He didn't know where north was or, it seemed, who he was.

He stopped two stairs from the bottom and looked into our eyes. We looked into his, hopefully. "I thought it over," he said. "And it is catralph . . . utterly catralph."

Then he ambled off the set. We really had to scramble. There was no finish to the show without him telling us what he had decided about his fortune, and we desperately wanted to know where the hell did that nonword *catralph* come from. We handled it with aplomb. There'd been bizarre incidents before, and this sort of thing was what you learned to take in stride in live television. You had to be ready for any mishap, and whatever came, able to work your way out of it.

Barbara Bel Geddes was a little older than we three young stars. She was the niece of the famous industrial designer Norman Bel Geddes, and she was a Broadway star. Later in her life, she played one of the lead roles in the TV series *Dallas*. Barbara didn't have a great deal of experience in live television, but she was doing a television show of high drama. At one point she had to run to her dressing room, and I mean run, take off her blouse, put on a strapless bra and a low-cut blouse, and rush back to the set. She barely made it during the dress rehearsal.

We were doing the live performance and came to that moment where Barbara rushed off the set and into her dressing room and furiously began the change. Apparently she became completely discombobulated and ran out of her dressing room and onto the set with no bra and no blouse. Tits akimbo! The costume lady, who was prepared for such extreme events, walked onto the set, threw a shawl over Barbara, and walked off, and the scene went on.

Once I was doing a New York City police drama. The bad guy, an actor and friend of mine named Eddie Rissien, and I were holed up on a set that replicated an apartment on the first floor of a brownstone building. The cops were outside, where the set was built to look like a street in Hell's Kitchen. Eddie and I weren't giving up to the police demands that we surrender, and there was going to be a gunfight. The cops on the street outside were extras in NYPD uniforms, which, as I remember, didn't fit them very well.

Before the dress rehearsal, Eddie asked to look at the shotgun and pistol he would be firing. As the propman showed them to him, Eddie said, "I'll be firing these in the dress rehearsal, right?"

"Nah, just fake it. I don't want to have to load them again," the propman said.

"But I need to know what's gonna happen when I fire them. I don't know how much of a charge is in them." The four extras in the NYPD uniforms were listening nervously to the conversation.

"Trust me," the propman said. "They'll work fine."

But Eddie persisted, and finally, the director agreed with him. In the dress rehearsal, when we got to the gunfight, Eddie started firing his shotgun at the police outside. The noise was deafening, and the explosion was so strong, the huge exterior wall detached itself from the rest of the set and started falling on the street, where the NYPD extras were. As they saw it descending toward them, they panicked. They ran off the set and out the door of the soundstage and down the street. When the assistant director found them, they were scared and shaking, no way they would come back. The assistant director retrieved their uniforms and had to round up four new extras. He had no time, we were about twenty minutes from going on the air, so he just pulled four guys in off the street.

On another occasion I played a woman who had fallen into a depressed and angry state and was thinking about ending her life. I sat at my dressing table, staring at myself in the mirror; heavy with emotion, I raised my pistol and shot point-blank at my image. The mirror exploded into little pieces, which flew back and buried themselves in my face. There wasn't anything to do, I went on with the rest of the show. By the end of it, my face had swelled to one and a half times its normal size. This was live television.

One last illustration of how primitive things were. I was in a show with Fay Bainter, a famous older actress at that time. We were sitting on her front porch in the evening. To make things look real, the propman walked by behind the camera, with a light in each hand to indicate a car was passing by.

As soon as *John Loves Mary* and *Happy Birthday* closed, I began working at the Old Nick on the Lower East Side. The Old Nick was half nightclub, half vaudeville house. It was a spawning ground for a number of young actors. Jack Lemmon worked there just before I did. The Old Nick showed old films, including a lot of silent films, and between screenings, they would have what they called olios. We, the performers, would dance, sing, and do anything to entertain the audience. It was a warm and inviting place, just pure performance.

One of the funniest acts was two men, Bob and Ray. One of them had me laughing till I couldn't control my bladder. One would interview the other on some completely insane premise. Ray started alone onstage, speaking into the microphone in a low voice, as if he didn't want to be heard by the people in the room, who had come to see the competition he was describing.

"Ladies and gentlemen, we're at the end of our final round of the Slow Talkers of America Championship—and I do believe . . . Yes, they're gesturing to me. We have our winner, and he's making his way toward our microphone now. And here he is . . . Well, good evening, Mr. Hornsacker. You faced some real competition tonight, and I know you must be a tad on the exhausted side. But tell me. How does it feel to be the new Slow Talkers of America champion?"

A long, long pause. "Um," Bob would say and leave a towering silence. Ray would stand admiringly by, watching the new champion show his stuff. "I . . . uh," Bob would add before another unbelievably long pause. "didn't . . . expect . . ."

Ray would show the first sign of tension in trying to have a conversation at this speed. "You didn't expect to . . ."

There would be another long pause, then sustained pauses between each word. "I . . . didn't . . . expect . . . the . . ."

Ray, feeling the strain, "You didn't expect what? That there would be so many competitors? Four instead of two? What was it that took you by surprise, Mr. Hornsacker?"

Again, interminable pauses. "Well . . . I . . . didn't . . . expect . . . that . . ."

"That, that, that what? Help us out here, Mr. Hornsacker. You've won the title. You can get out of first gear. What was it you didn't expect, please?"

After an unbearable pause, the first word. "Well . . . the . . ."

"The, the what? We have to know what." Ray was close to tearing his hair out, even closer to shooting Mr. Hornsacker. "We need a little more pace from you now, Mr. Cornwhacker."

"The . . . ferocity . . ." Super long pause.

"Ferocity?" Where the hell can you find ferocity in the Slow Talkers of America Championship? For God's sake, hurry. The cleaning crew comes in at two in the morning."

At this point, Bob would speak in a normal cadence. "The ferocity was in the eyes of my competitors. I've never seen such a vicious will to win."

The audience loved them. They'd take their bow and trot offstage.

Learning how to be spontaneous, how to start moving to the music or get up and sing or talk to the audience—those were valuable things I absorbed at the Old Nick. The days there were an important part of my theatrical training.

New York was different then. I walked all the way home one night from the Old Nick, on the Lower East Side, to where Hy lived (more about Hy later), on Eighty-seventh Street on upper Fifth Avenue, near the Metropolitan Museum Of Art. I walked the whole way without a suggestion of fear. It occurs to me as I look back that there were two possibilities: either New York wasn't dangerous in those days or I was just plain ignorant.

I think I was just plain ignorant. Here is another little

tale. There is a hotel on Broadway, between Forty-third and Forty-fourth streets, with a lobby that runs through the whole block. I believe it's the Edison. Not long, maybe three weeks, after I took my late night walk from the Old Nick to upper Fifth Avenue, at a little before noon, I was passing through the lobby of the Edison. Out of nowhere, a man rushed at me, grabbed me, and held me against a column. He then started grinding his pelvis into me. It didn't take him long to climax, and as soon as he did, he turned and strode away. So did I. He went his way, and I went mine.

It was curious. I felt no emotion during the mini-drama, not fear, not alarm. It happened, It was an interruption of the path I'd set for the day. End of story. But I had a sense of incompletion. There'd been no finale, no adios, no bowing to the audience and waving back to them as they applauded. On a smaller scale, the impetuous one might have tipped his hat to me and said a gracious thank-you for having borrowed my body. That was New York. You learned to walk the walk.

On an evening not long after, I jumped into a cab on Park Avenue to go downtown, to Forty-eighth Street. We barely got moving when the driver pulled out his wangy and started flogging it, trying to show it to me as he worked. At the first red light, I jumped out. That was New York. You learned to walk the walk.

More About the Actors Studio

I learned a lot at the Actors Studio, but I made enemies there as well as friends, the latter because I refused to take the "Method" seriously. I howled at the story Bette Davis told of how during the filming of *The Night of the Iguana* (1964), an actor took an entire day to figure out his motivation for removing his shoe. Her patience bursting into flame, Davis stood up and yelled, "Just take the god damn thing off! It's only a shoe!"

Stella Adler was a devoted practitioner of the "Method," and in her class one day was Marlon Brando. She told the students they were to be chickens and that an atom bomb was falling and would land in fifteen seconds. The improvisation began, and everyone ran around the room, showing different versions of hysteria. Except Brando. He sat still. When Stella asked him why, he said, "I'm a chicken. What do I know about atom bombs?"

Stella had a big influence on Marlon. Not only did she see the enormous talent that lay within him, but she took him into her world, her home, her family. Marlon became

very close to Ellen, Stella's daughter, and their relationship lasted all through Marlon's life.

Marlon asked me out several times, but I didn't go. I
felt he'd want to take me to his apartment and probably it
wouldn't be clean, and I'd find it disgusting. Also, he was
after every girl that twitched, and I didn't want to be one of
the multitude.

About five years later, we met at a party in Beverly Hills.
Marlon was going to play the lead in the 1956 MGM movie
The Teahouse of the August Moon, and Burgess Meredith, a close
friend of ours, was doing the play onstage in Los Angeles.
Burgess gave a *Teahouse* party for Marlon and him and invited George and me. At the time, Marlon was at the very
peak of his stardom, his power, his charisma, and everybody in the industry wanted to be at that party. Marlon
and two girlfriends, one an attractive woman, who was his
assistant, and the other a Jack Cole dancer, beautiful and
Japanese who glided along beside Marlon, arrived late. All
the Hollywood moguls, movie stars, and power brokers
were mesmerized as this trio made their entrance. Marlon
was cordial as Burgess introduced him to the other guests,
cordial but also a bit removed. Truly, there was a godlike
aura around Marlon. It showed in his behavior and everyone's response to him. The women did everything but
curtsy.

After the introductions and brief chats, Marlon left
the crowd and came over to George and me. I remember
the moment with perfect clarity.

"Well, Cloris, Clorass," Marlon said. "What have you
been doing?"

"Having babies, Marlon," I smiled.

"How many?"

"We have two boys."

"Gonna have any more?"

"Maybe. Ask George."

Marlon turned to George. "Gonna have any more babies, George?"

George answered with an old burlesque line. "Not sure, Marlon. Haven't found out what's causing it."

Marlon chuckled, not so much at the joke as at the unpredictability of George's response. At that moment a chord was struck between them.

"I always thought Cloris was the most talented one at the Studio," Marlon said. "That made me curious as to who she'd wind up marrying. What's it like? Pretty madcap, George?"

"Madcap, madhouse. Something with *mad* in it," replied George. He smiled and put his arm around me.

Marlon appraised me for a moment, then spoke to George. "Kazan had us wear work clothes to class because a lot of times, he'd have us get down on the floor to do an exercise. One day he told us to lie down and be a reptile. I got on my stomach and was going to be a monitor lizard when I looked over and there was Cloris beside me, wearing a beautiful pink suit, high heels, silk stockings, ready for a swanky evening with the rich crowd."

"How was my improvisation, Marlon? Do you remember? Did I do a good lizard?" I asked.

Marlon waited a moment before he answered. "Spellbinding. I remember being impressed at how you invested in it, how you made that reptile real. You held nothing back. You actually became a lizard."

I couldn't pass up that opportunity. I dropped to the floor and did my lizard imitation with the same conviction I'd shown at the Actors Studio. It pretty well stopped conversation. The guests couldn't imagine what Marlon Brando had said to that woman that would have her get down on the floor, on her stomach, and, and . . . behave like a lizard.

At the end of the evening, Marlon said, "What are you guys doing tomorrow night?"

"Nothing special," I said and turned to George. "Right?"

"Right. Nothing planned," replied George.

"I've got a date with Anna Magnani, and I know she's gonna try to fuck me," Marlon said. "And that is truly the last thing in the world I want to happen, so can you two come along, give me some protection?"

We laughed. "Yes, we'll ride shotgun," George said.

Anna Magnani was a famous Italian actress known for her earthiness, her passion, her unrestrained sexuality. All of it was on display during our dinner the next evening. And Marlon had guessed correctly. Right from the shrimp cocktail, Anna had him in her sexual sights.

When we left the restaurant, Marlon drove, Anna beside him, and George and I in the backseat. It was rowdy. We were all under the influence of the wine we'd had at dinner. To start things off, Marlon farted loudly, which he could do at will, then rolled up all the windows so we had to suffer the stench. During the frivolity, Anna moved close to Marlon and put her hand on his thigh. Marlon's eyes found George's in the rearview mirror. "See what I mean?" his look said.

"Marlon, why we don't a let them offa to have a coffee somewhere and a we go somewhere else?" Anna murmured. "Maybe we go to you a house."

Marlon shot George another look in the rearview mirror, "What'd I tell you?" "No, I have to drop you at the hotel, then drive them home," Marlon responded.

"*Perchè*? Why? Where they a live?" asked Anna.

"Mojave," Marlon said. We broke up in the backseat.

"*Che*? Mo what? I never hear of this a place."

George chimed in. "You know, I think Anna's right, Marlon. You kids ought to be alone. It's written all over you what you want to do, drop us off, and we'll get a cab."

Marlon's eyes bulged as he looked in the rearview mirror. "You shit," he mouthed in a silent scream, but he also couldn't keep from laughing.

"What he's a say?" Anna wanted to know.

"He's saying he knows I'm going to cut him a new asshole because of the suggestions he's making."

Anna didn't respond. By this time she was in a state of total confusion.

Ultimately, Marlon dropped us at our car, and the next afternoon he was at our house to tell us in great detail how he had outdueled the overzealous Signora Magnani. He was at his acting best; he re-created her lunges and his ripostes in hilarious detail. These times when Marlon was improvising on human behavior were when his talent shone most brightly to me. Anyone watching was jolted into laughter. So often at these moments, I sighed in despair that we were the only ones there. The whole world should have been watching Marlon and George do their shtick.

With all the joking about Anna, I learned something about being a woman from her that night. She was always completely herself. She didn't try to do what others thought was appropriate for her, didn't try to be what others considered beautiful. She had a slight mustache and was in no way apologetic about it. All of her was there to see; the world could like her or not, but she would not be anyone other than who she was. In that one evening with her, I saw a woman who gave free rein to her passions, put no barriers in front of her feelings and aspirations. In the track meet of this life, Anna Magnani ran with everything she had.

The four of us went to dinner the following night, and that was the beginning of the long friendship between George and Marlon. George was trying to get a foothold in television as a producer and director and as Woody Guthrie says in his song, he was "havin' some hard travelin'." Ironically, almost every evening, when he came home from his appointments, his efforts, America's biggest movie star was in the living room of our little house, playing with our kids, waiting for George to arrive. Sometimes we'd all have something I prepared for dinner, sometimes the three of us would go to a restaurant, and sometimes the two of them would take off. They'd drive up the coast, sometimes as far as Santa Barbara, and come back as late as two in the morning. Talking, they were always talking.

We did family things together. Our son Georgie and

Marlon's son Christian were the same age, so they saw a lot of each other. One Christmas holiday we teamed up with Marlon and rented Henry Kaiser's house in Hawaii. It was a spacious, palatial Hawaiian home built for parties, with a seemingly endless granite floor. All the chairs, high backs, barrel backs, were on rollers, so the vast living room became the site for an ongoing game of Dodge 'Em. Mr. Kaiser's finely chosen chairs zoomed across his fine granite floor at all hours and at high speeds.

During our stay in Hawaii, we chartered a yacht for New Year's Eve and sailed off the coast of Oahu to see Honolulu all lit up. It was royal. We adults sipped champagne, and the children gazed in awe at the fireworks and prowled around every corner of the vessel.

Several times we took the boys down to Marlon's atoll, Tetiaroa, which lies forty miles off Tahiti. These too were special events. An atoll is a lagoon out in the middle of the ocean, surrounded by a coral reef. The lagoon at Tetiaroa is about a mile in diameter and is shallow compared to the ocean; its color is a light azure, which makes it stand out from the deep blue of the sea around it. Inside the lagoon are small islands that rise only two or three feet above the surface.

One evening, as we were about to sit down to dinner, we noticed that Georgie and Christian were not there. We looked around and couldn't find them anywhere. Finally, wide eyed and wringing wet, they walked out of the lagoon. They'd been playing out in the middle, and they'd watched several sharks patrolling, one of them sixteen feet long. Focused on the ocean life, they lost track of time, suddenly night fell. That was a whole different world. They were frightened to get off the coral heads they were standing on and start to swim to our island; they were certain that if they did, one of those sharks would come up alongside and bite off a leg. So they stood on the coral heads, getting colder and more fearful. Finally, they decided they had to risk it. They jumped off their roosts and broke the international record for nine-year-olds sprinting across the lagoon of an atoll. They filled the dinnertime with stories of what they'd seen while inspecting the large lagoon.

On another occasion on Tetiaroa, Marlon had a serious talk with Bryan about his drug use. Marlon had a special affection for Bryan. He saw himself, a rebel, in Bryan. Bryan was a drummer, and Marlon gave him his personal set of conga drums. On this occasion Marlon said he'd give Bryan one hundred thousand dollars if he'd stop taking drugs for six months. If Bryan violated the agreement, the payment would drop to seventy-five thousand dollars. If he violated it again, the payment would drop to fifty thousand and so on. Like all such well-meaning schemes, it didn't work. But Marlon's concern for Bryan didn't stop; he always kept in touch with him.

Often on weekends we brought the boys up to Marlon's house on Mulholland Drive in Beverly Hills. He had a large swimming pool, and all of us would jump in, splash each other, and create mayhem. Marlon and George would throw the boys up in the air to see who could send them highest. Afterward, we'd have a hearty barbecue or a fine French dinner, which Marlon would have brought up from a restaurant he liked on Ventura Boulevard.

Despite all the fun, I was concerned about the kind of father Marlon was being to Christian. I didn't see an enormous amount of it firsthand but the reports were that Christian had had a sad, if not terrifying, childhood. He was the tortured ground on which the bitter custody battles between Marlon and his former wife Anna Kashfi were fought.

It was painful to recall Marlon and Anna's romantic beginning. One night early in their marriage, the four of us were going out to dinner. George and I came by to pick them up, and Marlon and we were in the living room waiting for Anna to join us. She appeared at the top of the stairs and started down. She was positively breathtaking, young and beautiful, with all the meaning those words can carry. But even then, the acrimony between them had begun, the dinner was filled with their digs at each other.

I watched Christian grow through the years, saw the results of parental neglect, and witnessed the beginning of his drug taking. I saw how he learned to manipulate Marlon. And Marlon could be manipulated because he was lazy. He didn't want to change the course of his life; he literally didn't want to get out of the chair to be an attentive parent. When Christian started smoking marijuana, Marlon wanted him to do it at their home on Mulholland Drive. His attitude was that if Christian was going to smoke pot, he'd rather he did it in the house so he'd know where he was. He didn't say anything about getting Christian to stop. And if he knew marijuana was a gateway drug that could lead Christian to deeper addiction, he didn't tell

Christian about it. He didn't try to interdict the marijuana use.

Christian didn't have the compulsion, the drive, that Marlon had, but he had inherited Marlon's ability to analyze the behavior of others and use that knowledge to control them. As he grew up, Christian used that talent to analyze his father, to assess his moods, so he'd know what approach to take when he wanted money or something else from Marlon. Whereas Marlon could stun the world with his creations Terry Malloy and Stanley Kowalski, his son could, with equal dexterity, exploit Marlon's lack of discipline and weak resolve to perform the role of parent.

Both Christian's life and death were high tragedy to me. What happened when he died is still a mystery. Apparently, there was considerable wrangling about who had the right to claim the body. Christian's remains lay in the county morgue, as I understand it, till near the time when, if no one made a legitimate claim to them, the county would dispose of them.

Apparently, Anna didn't have the money to claim her son's body, and there was endless maneuvering by an assortment of people to claim it. Finally, as I heard, Christian's body, or his cremated remains, I'm not sure which, ended up in Oregon. Such was the inglorious end of the complex, difficult life of Marlon Brando's son, or at least as I understand it from the jumbled accounts I heard.

I don't know how Marlon stood up under the emotional assaults that came to him. His daughter Cheyenne, pregnant with the child of Dag Drollet, whom Christian killed that awful night at Marlon's house, committed suicide by hanging herself in her mother's house in Tahiti. It was staggering news to me. Terrible questions filled my mind. What fires inside her had prompted such a tragic act?—And how would a Tahitian girl even know the mechanics of successfully hanging herself? Neither Marlon nor Christian attended Cheyenne's funeral. I think, in Marlon's case, wisdom was the better part of valor. A lawsuit had been filed against him by Dag Drollet's family, alleging he bore some responsibility for Dag's death.

There was one aspect of George and Marlon's relationship that was troublesome to me, and I think that it affected our marriage negatively. Not only did they spend evenings together, they talked endlessly on the phone. It was more Marlon than George. Marlon liked nothing better than to lie on his bed, phone in hand, and talk about whatever came into his mind: the electric power in eels, Shakespeare's keen view of human behavior, the way Sugar Ray Robinson could flatten you with either hand, whatever. Most of all, he loved to talk about those things with George. I thought George's mistake was to allow Marlon to use up so much of his time, time I thought he could have better spent doing other things.

I can't say that overall and through the years, I was close to Marlon. I think he saw me as an obstacle to his having the relationship he wanted with George. Marlon was unpredictable to me. The worst thing that happened between us came right after Christian killed Cheyenne's boyfriend in Marlon's house. I was sad for Marlon, but it didn't occur to me that he'd like to hear from me. I imagined the whole world was sending condolences and trying to speak to him, and the absence of anything from me would not be of particular notice. And yet Marlon told George he would never forgive me for not contacting him after the tragedy had happened in his life. And he didn't. Whenever we spoke after that, he was extremely chilly.

I remember wondering when their friendship first started, why George and Marlon would be friends. They seemed so different from each other. George was a college graduate, while Marlon didn't finish high school. They both went to military school. Marlon was thrown out of his, George was the highest-ranking officer at his. Both in military school and in the navy, George learned an ethic that he lived by. Marlon didn't seem to me to have any moral commitment.

Later on I did see why they became so close. They had their own humor, their own way of observing life, they competed in wit and in sports. Fathers were a frequent focus of their talks. Marlon hated his father, and George didn't have one, so they became paternal to each other. They did what fathers do: they gave counsel and encouragement; they rescued each other in the dark times, when one was failing and frightened; and they shared a fascination with the mystery of human existence. Theirs was a fraternity of two. It had no other members.

Three days before Marlon died, he called George. He was in a very emotional state. These were Marlon's words during that phone call to George. He was in tears when he spoke them. "I just wanted you to know I love you, Georgie. I'd take a bullet for you. I've said it before. If you had a cunt, we'd have been married a long time ago." George came to my home to tell me about the call before he went to see Marlon during what turned out to be the last twenty-four hours of Marlon's life. George wanted us to look back together at the long road we'd traveled with Marlon, one that we'd started down that night when Marlon said to me, "Well, Cloris, Clorass. What have you been doing?"

We laughed and were solemn as we looked back at the direction our three lives had followed right up to this moment. Then George left me to spend the afternoon and evening with Marlon. Shortly after George left Marlon's house, Marlon was taken to the hospital, where he died.

Let me end this section with these words. Marlon, if you're listening, I want you to know I felt the deepest compassion for what happened to Christian, you, and Cheyenne. I remember our salad days at the Actors Studio, the shining young things we were then, so brimming with anticipation, so unaware of the startling events that lay ahead. Imperfect you might have been—though probably not more imperfect than any of the rest of us—but nobody else at that time of our lives had that thunder in his acting, that power inside himself to portray another human being that you had.

I digressed from talking about the Actors Studio, so let me go back. The Studio was a spawning place for both the wonderful and the weird. Here's a typical example of the odd things that happened there. Elia Kazan put a lot of emphasis on how to use objects. As an exercise, he had us pantomime using an imaginary object. One actor got up to pantomime peeling a banana—without the banana. He got deep into it; he studiously pulled each section of the skin down from the top of the banana, totally focused as he proceeded. Suddenly he looked up and, with a slight tremble in his voice, said, "My God, I can actually smell it!" He thought his improvisation was so real, it had actually produced a banana smell.

It was me. I was sitting in the second row, eating a banana. The poor guy was heartbroken, especially as the rest of the class laughed so hard, they were in tears.

In those days, the Actors Studio was magic. Kazan had assembled the best young actors in America. Each was talented and had been taught to be free in the use of his or her talent, each had imagination and energy and discipline, and each was exciting to work with. Jack Warden was one of the best. I loved Jack. We did scenes together that lifted our fellow actors out of their chairs. We loved each other. After we left the Studio, I didn't see much of Jack. We were both having good careers in Los Angeles, and only occasionally did our paths cross. But on those few occasions, the spark was rekindled, our brief talks would be lit again with the energy we'd had when we were doing those scenes at the Studio. I miss Jack.

Julie Harris was another exceptional talent. I saw her for the first time the day I came through the front door to try out for the Actors Studio. This poor little skinny girl was sitting in the corner, and I thought, *Oh, if I could just take her home with me and fatten her up*. Julie always stayed thin, but there was such transcendent power in her acting, you didn't notice how big or little she was. Her greatest triumph to me was her performance as the little girl in *The Member of the Wedding,* in which she starred with Ethel Waters both on stage and in the film.

At the Actors Studio, we had a dance class once a week. After one session, Julie and I were naked, about to get in the shower, and she said, "If I had your tits, I could rule the world." That coming out of little Julie Harris was shock and awe. It was unusual for her to say "darn" or "damn," let alone something as raunchy as that. Julie was, for the most part, a serious actress, a tasteful woman. Those are the words that come to me when I remember Julie.

In 1951 Burgess Meredith and I were set to star in *I Am a Camera,* a play written by John Van Druten and based on Christopher Isherwood's *The Berlin Stories.* The leading character is Sally Bowles, the part I would play. Mr. Van Druten asked if Burgess and I would come to his apartment and read the play. We said, "Yes, of course," and met in his handsome apartment overlooking the East River.

There is a delicate scene where Sally Bowles talks about having an abortion. I played the scene lightly, as if I were taking the event in stride, with no great emotional involvement. When we finished reading the scene, Mr. Van Druten was concerned: he thought the critics would not understand the scene if it were played that way.

What he didn't see was how Burgess had reacted. Burgess had noticed that I only *appeared* to be treating the issue lightly, actually I was masking the fear and sorrow inside me. Burgess and I tried to explain that the way I was playing the scene would be far more interesting than if I broke down in sobs. Van Druten didn't buy it; he thought the critics would slam the play if the scene was done that way. I knew I had made the right choice in playing the scene, but that incident gave me the first inkling that maybe I should not be doing the play.

In another scene, I had to prepare and down a hang-over drink with a raw egg in it, plus something that tasted like alum. I knew I couldn't drink that thing once, let alone nine times a week, in front of an audience. Then a miracle happened. Just as I was thinking that, Julie Harris popped into my mind, and I said to Van Druten, "You know who could do this part really well? Julie Harris." That started the recasting. That was how Julie got the lead role in *I Am a Camera*. And that role made her a star.

Burgess and I worked together again, he as the direc-tor, I as the leading woman in a 1951 play by S. N. Behr-man called *Let Me Hear the Melody!* Anthony Quinn played the male lead, and also in the cast were some of Broadway's finest actors. The scenes were highly charged, and these talented actors poured their energy into them.

More than once during rehearsals, things got out of control, the actors arguing fiercely with each other, even getting into a major harangue with Burgess. We had fold-ing chairs on stage to indicate sofas and other furniture. One afternoon, when emotions were raging, Tony Quinn picked up one of the folding chairs and hurled it out into the audience. It hit row twelve first, then bounced across the tops of several more rows before coming to a tangled, bent, awkward halt. If it had hit someone—and it could have, since the author of the play and a handful of others were spread throughout the first four rows—it would have done some real damage. The funny thing was that that moment of violence didn't change anything. Tony and the actor he'd been sparring with, J. Edward Bromberg, went on arguing just as explosively.

Let Me Hear the Melody! was a good play, with fine writing, but it never settled down into the drama it could've been. The producers abandoned the production before we even left town.

Back to the Actors Studio. Annie Jackson, who was married to Eli Wallach, was another excellent actress. One afternoon Kazan had the women improvise on this situation: We had five minutes to spend with our husband, who was in prison. What would we do? I knew what I would do. I'd climb into his arms, burst into tears, and stay there for the full five minutes.

Annie Jackson did something very different. She came in, hugged and kissed her husband, then sat down, got out a piece of paper, and began going down a list of things she had to tell him about: money, the children, their home, his parents. When she finished, she looked at him again with such love, you couldn't help but cry. What she'd done demanded skillful acting. She'd shown that you could do several things, and not just stay on one line, in one mood. You could start one way, then move to something else, and then come back to where you'd started and have it be even more compelling.

The Studio changed radically when Lee Strasberg came in with his acting group. Suddenly, it was the Tower of Babel; everyone seemed to be speaking different languages.

Strasberg was always dear to me—he practically licked my neck—but he was cruel to actors who I thought were just as good as I was. Sometimes I'd do absolutely nothing, and he'd rave about it.

A critical moment came for me when Marty Balsam and I were preparing a scene from *Othello*. He was the Moor and I was his wife, Desdemona. I loved Marty. There was a talented man. Before we went on, another actor, Joe Sullivan, did an extended monologue. Strasberg hated it, and he raked Joe over the coals, tore him to pieces. It was horrible and grossly unfair.

Marty and I started our scene, the one at the end of the play, where Desdemona is sleeping and Othello comes in to kill her, because he believes she's having an affair with the captain of his guard. I got on the bed and acted as if I were asleep. Marty, as Othello, moved worriedly, indecisively, around the room, considering whether he could actually kill his sleeping wife. "Put out the light," Othello says, looking at the torch burning over Desdemona's bed, "and then put out the light," meaning he would then choke her to death.

Marty delivered the rest of the speech. Staring at the burning torch, he said, "If I quench thee, thou flaming minister, I can again thy former light restore, should I repent me." Then he looked at me, Desdemona, and as he studied my sleeping face, he said, "But once put out thy light, thou cunning'st pattern of excelling nature, I know not where is that Promethean heat that can thy light relume."

Beautifully portraying Othello's awful dilemma, Marty

then stood still. Then he went up to the front of the stage and said, "I can't kill her." Everybody laughed. The scene had become so real to him, he couldn't go on with it.

When the laughter subsided, Strasberg started to discuss the scene with the class. He began by raving about me—and I had done nothing but get into bed. I was furious and disgusted, especially since Strasberg had been so unfair to the actor who had done his monologue just before us. That decided me. I left the Actors Studio that day and never went back.

I didn't leave just because of Strasberg. I really felt I had gotten all I could out of being there. The Studio was changing as new members came in, and Kazan was less a part of the everyday operation. I'd had all the best of it.

Wait. There was one other incident that had something to do with my leaving. One afternoon, at the end of our session, Kazan asked if I'd like to have lunch the next day. It seemed an absolutely splendid idea, I responded with an enthusiastic yes. We met at the perfect restaurant, Longchamps, on Fifty-seventh Street. It was a Saturday afternoon, and the whole ambience was out of a picture book. The cuisine was superb. We enjoyed spectacular lobster and flagons of a crisp white wine. This was wonderful. I was having lunch with the giant of the American theater. Then Kazan made a suggestion that he and I should go somewhere and be alone, and spend the rest of the day together. It was an out-and-out proposition. The emotion I felt was sadness. He was my teacher. I had put him on an altar, and here he was, stepping down off that sacred place.

I said no, I didn't want to do that. That ended the meal; he paid the check and we went our separate ways.

There is an irony attached to this tale. Kazan always urged us not to go to Hollywood. He said we should stay and be a part of the New York theater. I didn't see him again after that lunch for probably five years. Our reunion took place at a party—in Hollywood. Kazan had himself forgotten his counsel about the sanctity of our profession and the obligation to practice it in New York. He was now at the center of the Hollywood scene.

Those days at the Studio; those improvs that stretched our imaginations; those friendships; those efforts to create, to be truthful; the whole colorful, demanding panorama of the days at the Actors Studio will forever be alive in my mind. Whenever I run into someone who was there when I was, there's a particular animation. We laugh and cry about that phenomenal experience, and underneath, what we're really saying to each other is, "Those were the good old days."

I want to interject something. It's personal, and I don't recommend it to everybody. It's that I don't associate money with acting. Acting is fun; it isn't work to me. I'm happy and excited when I'm acting, and that is the reward. I used to be profligate with money; I'd spend thousands of dollars on clothes to be the prettiest girl wherever I was. I wasn't the prettiest girl, but I wanted to be, and I tried to be.

I'd go to Bergdorf Goodman—they knew me, because I was there all the time—and they'd bring out their prettiest dresses. I'd pick the ones I liked, and if they didn't happen to be my size, the store was happy to alter them for me. As I got a bit older, all that changed, and thank God, it did. I do things differently now.

It's part of the rule book in Hollywood that you don't wear the same dress to two premieres. It's not a law enacted by the state legislature, but it might as well be, no one violates the commandment. Now I have a stylist I work with, Mike Sam, who, whenever I am going to a formal occasion, brings me two or three possible gowns. He knows my taste, and they are all good choices. I pick one, I use it for the occasion, then return it. Everything works out perfectly. The system is good economically. It's a lot less costly to have Mike find the right dress for me to borrow than to buy one each time I'm going to a formal occasion.

I think what an actress wears is important. It's important when she's performing a role, and it's important when she's out in the city. It's good for an actress to establish her look, her style, so it's a recognizable part of her.

More On Acting

I said at the beginning that I wasn't going to write my book in chapters. That also meant I wouldn't always set things down in a chronological line—as evidenced by what I've written so far.

Actors have to submerge themselves in their roles, lose their own identity, and actually become the character they're playing. They must think, eat, drink, and go to the bathroom as the character does. That can bring confusion to life.

For instance, in the 1971 film *The Last Picture Show*, which is based on a novel of the same name by Larry McMurtry, I played Ruth Popper, a spare, lean woman who lives an emotionally barren life in Texas. She is married to the high school football coach who is always away and, it seems, probably gay. That is Ruth Popper's life on the outside. Inside of her is a full-fledged female who wistfully retains the hope that romance might yet come her way. There were no frills either in the production or in my performance. The film was shot in black and white, and I wore no make-up.

Being Ruth Popper as her dormant emotions are awakened by a boy in his late teens was a deeply human experience. It radiated through my life. In preparing for the filming and during it, I not only came to look, walk, and talk like that sensually undernourished woman, but to become her. The rewards, both personal and professional, were extravagant. I won the Oscar for that performance.

I didn't read or audition for the role. The producers called my agent and said they wanted me to play the part. Their "firm offer," as it's called in the business, included where and when I'd be working and what the compensation would be. My agent brought the offer and the script to me. I read the script and told him I'd like to do the part.

Peter Bogdanovich was the director, and the preproduction process began with a reading of the script at his house. On that first occasion, Bogdanovich said something surprising: he thought Ellen Burstyn and Eileen Brennan and I were interchangeable, we could all play each other's parts. He asked Ellen first which part she would like to play. He said he thought it should be Ruth Popper. Ellen said no. She didn't want that role, so it came back to me. In truth, I would have been happy with any of the three roles, though I did like the part of Ruth Popper best.

Soon the production was under way. As we moved through the weeks Ellen and I became very close. Jeff Bridges, who played the part of Duane, proved to be not only a terrific actor but a wonderful man. All us ladies in the cast loved him and were attracted to him. It was my impression that Timothy Bottoms, who played my teenage lover, didn't really want to be in the picture. He had just done the film *Johnny Got His Gun*, and that was the kind of role he wanted, not this one. He wasn't part of us; he would come in and do a scene and then be gone. Rumors were, I don't know if they were true, that he was smoking a lot of pot.

Polly Platt, Peter's then-wife, contributed greatly to the success of the picture. As the production designer, she was meticulous in the selection of wardrobe elements. From what she presented, I chose my coat, my hat, my bra, and my little white panties, and I feel strongly that these things were mine, Ruth Popper's. Polly's wardrobe helped me to know exactly who I was.

During the filming, Ellen, Eileen, and I became involved with the people we met in the restaurant in town called the Golden Rooster. We'd eat there almost every night and hear their real life stories. One day the owner of the restaurant began ranting that her lover had left her. She was married, and we thought she was upset because her husband had gone away, but that wasn't the case at all. It was her lover whom she was publicly moaning for. That sort of story was going on all around us in that little town. It was fascinating because we were actually portraying those people. Larry McMurtry had written his novel, *The Last Picture Show*, about the very people we were talking to.

Peter Bogdanovich was a different kind of director. I wasn't used to the way he directed. He'd come over and say some of my lines quietly in my ear. Good directors don't give actors line readings, but I realized as we went along

Peter didn't mean to be giving me line readings. He wanted to suggest the quality of the scene. Bogdanovich was good. He knew what he was doing, and he knew what he wanted.

When we shot my major scene, the long one that, in my opinion, earned me the Oscar, Peter printed the first take. I wanted to shoot it again; I thought I could do at least the first part better. Peter said, "No, you're going to get the Academy Award for that scene." I thought, *Yeah, sure.* I didn't know I'd done it that well. Acting is so subjective. Sometimes you think you were splendid, and you get lukewarm reactions; sometimes you're almost rueful at what you did, and people tell you how brilliant you were. Anyway, I didn't think I'd done that scene as well as I could have.

I replayed the scene while I was in bed this morning, and I believe I did it better. Particularly, I did the early part better, where I say to Timothy, who's just arrived at my house, "I wouldn't have been in my bathrobe. I would have been dressed hours ago."

The night I won the Academy Award was one extended thrill. I couldn't have imagined that after accepting it, I wouldn't work for a full year. I don't know why that happened, whether it was because, as some have suggested, producers thought I'd be too expensive, or because I didn't have a manager at the time, or whether it was the "Oscar curse." A story comes to mind about the "Oscar curse." Many years ago, after winning the Best Actress Oscar for her performance as O-Lan in *The Good Earth*, after enjoying the applause and the standing ovation, Luise Rainer didn't

1934: The Leachman sisters: Claiborne, Mary, and Cloris.

1936: Cloris awakens to her life as a performer.

1943: Cloris in downtown Des Moines, Iowa after school.

1943: A short film titled "Women At War" (WAC's). Cloris's character writes home to her mother.

1946: Cloris plays piano for Claiborne and Mary. Her mother, Cloris Sr., knows that her first daughter is going to hit the big time. Cloris has on the dress she'll wear for her first trip to New York.

1946: Chicago—Cloris hits all the hot spots in town.

1946: Atlantic City, on a float in the Miss America Parade.
Cloris dons her college formal dress as Miss Chicago.
(Courtesy of the Miss America Organization.)

1947: New York—Cloris understudies seven roles simultaneously for two plays, "John Loves Mary" and "Happy Birthday."

1948: Kraft TV, New York. *(Courtesy of NCBU Photo Bank)*

1947: Cloris Leachman Sr. in front of the family garage in Des Moines, Iowa.

1948: In back: Cloris Sr., Cloris, and her father, Buck.
In front: Claiborne and Mary.

1948: Somewhere in New York.

1950: Cloris and Katharine Hepburn on Broadway in Shakespeare's "As You Like It" at the Cort Theater. *(Courtesy of the Billy Rose Theatre Division, The New York Public Library for the Performing Arts, Astor, Lenox and Tilden Foundations.)*

1950: Katharine Hepburn, Ernest Graves, and Cloris on Broadway in Shakespeare's "As You Like It." *(Courtesy of the Billy Rose Theatre Division, The New York Public Library for the Performing Arts, Astor, Lenox and Tilden Foundations.)*

April 19, 1953: Cloris pins the boutonnière on her father
before her wedding to George Englund.

April 19, 1953: Cloris and George Englund are married.

April 19, 1953: Cloris and George celebrate their marriage. Cloris is four and half months pregnant with Adam.

April 19, 1953: Buck, Cloris, George, George's mother Mabel, and Cloris Sr. share a toast to the new couple.

1956: Cloris frolicking in Palm Beach, while George scouted Asia for his film "The Ugly American."

1959: During a play directed by her mother-in-law, Mabel Albertson.

1960: George Englund with sons Adam, Bryan, and George Jr. by the railroad tracks on Sepulveda in West Los Angeles. Gabby, the family Doberman, is panting on the left. *(Photo by Cloris Leachman.)*

1964: Adam, Bryan, Cloris, Morgan, George Jr., and George Sr. at their Rockingham house in Brentwood.

1965: Morgan, Adam, George Jr., Cloris, and Bryan *(below)*.
Adam arrives at LAX after location scouting in Africa with his father.

Claiborne, Mary, and Cloris with their maternal aunt, Lucille Ross.

1970-1977: Cloris as Phyllis Lindstrom on "The Mary Tyler Moore Show" and her spinoff series, "Phyllis." *(Copyright © 1975 Twentieth Century Fox Television. All Rights Reserved.)*

1971: Cloris wins the Oscar for Best Supporting Actress for her performance as Ruth Popper in Peter Bogdanovich's film "The Last Picture Show." *(Copyright © Academy of Motion Picture Arts and Sciences.)*

1974: Cloris, as Frau Blucher, shares a tender moment with The Monster (Peter Boyle) in Mel Brooks's masterpiece, "Young Frankenstein." *(Copyright © 1974 Twentieth Century Fox. All Rights Reserved.)*

1974: Cloris whispers off-camera to Gene Wilder (Dr. Frankenstein) in "Young Frankenstein." *(Copyright © 1974 Twentieth Century Fox. All Rights Reserved)*

7300-79

1973: Cloris plays The Lady in Red in the American classic "Dillinger."

1972: A rare shot of the whole family, taken at the Mandeville house:
Bryan, Cloris, George Jr., Morgan, Adam, Dinah, and George Sr.
(Work for hire.)

1974: Bryan and Cloris at a restaurant in L.A. *(Work for hire.)*

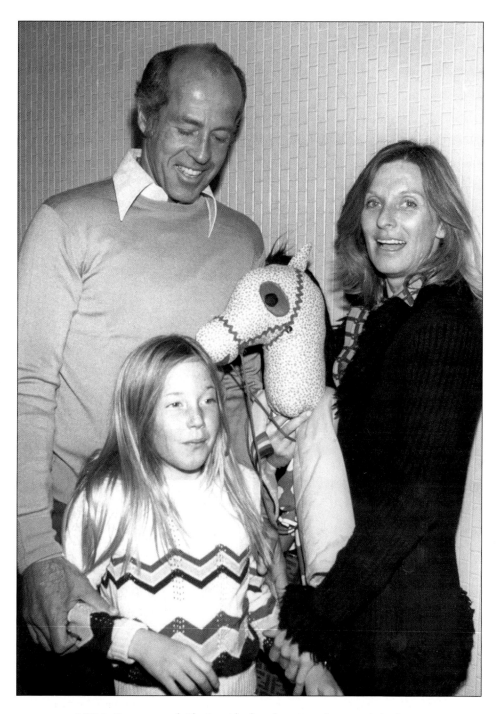

1974: George and Cloris with daughter Dinah. *(Work for hire.)*

1975: Cloris immersed in character as Old Mam Hawes in the TV movie "A Girl Named Sooner." *(Courtesy of NBCU Photo Bank.)*

1977: Cloris as the unforgettable Nurse Diesel in "High Anxiety." *(Copyright © 1977 Twentieth Century Fox. All Rights Reserved.)*

1977 Cloris is flanked by Harvey Korman and Mel Brooks at the Institute for the Very Very Nervous in "High Anxiety." *(Copyright © 1977 Twentieth Century Fox. All Rights Reserved.)*

1981: Cloris in her lovely Mandeville home kitchen.

1986-1988: Cloris follows Charlotte Rae as surrogate mother Beverly Ann Stickle for the girls on "The Facts of Life." *(Courtesy of NBCU Photo Bank.)*

Portia and her son Braden. Cloris's first granddaughter and great-grandson from her second son, Bryan.
(Photo Credit: Rand De Mattei.)

1989: Morgan, George, and Adam Englund with their respective daughters, Anabel, Skye, and Arielle.

1987: Animal lover Cloris gets to know the locals in Australia.

1989: Cloris displays her range during the first reading of the play "Grandma Moses," playing Grandma Moses at forty-five years old *(left)* and one hundred *(right)*.

1993: Cloris as Granny after receiving shock treatment in the feature film version of the TV series "The Beverly Hillbillies." *(Copyright © 1993 Twentieth Century Fox. All Rights Reserved.)*

1996: Cloris won an Emmy for Guest Starring Actress as Aunt Ethel Mooster in the TV series "Promised Land." *(Courtesy of CBS Broadcasting, Inc. All Rights Reserved.)*

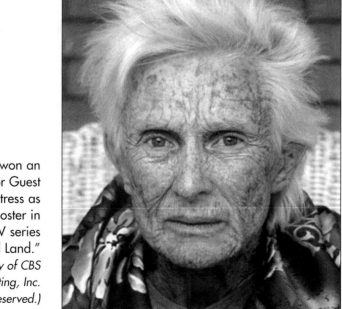

1996: Cloris poses nude on the cover of Alternative Health magazine,
adorned with fruits and vegetables body-painted by Rusty Arena.
(Courtesy of InnoVision Health Media, Inc.)

2004: Cloris plays Evelyn Wright, Tea Leoni's mother, in Jim Brooks's film "Spanglish." *(Copyright © 2004 by Columbia Pictures Industries. All Rights Reserved.)*

2006: Cloris as Great Gam Gam in the comedy "Beerfest."
(Copyright © 2006 by Warner Bros. Entertainment, Inc. All Rights Reserved.)

2006: Cloris's sons, daughter-in-law and grandchildren. *From left to right:* Morgan, Jackson, Skye, George Jr., Adam's wife Victoria, Arielle, Adam, and Anabel.

2007: Cloris with granddaughter Hallelujah. *(Jaimee Itagaki)*

2007: Cloris in front of the Coliseum in Rome, with granddaughter Skye.

2006: The graduation episode and series finale for "Malcolm in the Middle." Cloris received three Emmys and six nominations for her recurring role as the evil Grandma Ida. *(Copyright 2006 by Twentieth Century Fox Television. All Rights Reserved.)*

2006: Cloris's eightieth birthday in Malibu.

2008: Cloris Leachman with Corky Ballas on *Dancing With the Stars*.
(George Englund, Jr.)

GRAND MARSHAL

2008: Cloris is announced as Grand Marshall of the 120th Anniversary of The Tournament of Roses.

work again for months. It was okay with me that I wasn't working. I would've been happy either way.

After *The Last Picture Show*, complexity came into my life. On the heels of that role I joined *The Mary Tyler Moore Show* to play Phyllis, a woman as far from Ruth Popper as you could meet in a round-the-world journey. For three years, I lived as Phyllis, the high-handed zany who saw the world as responsible for quickly meeting her needs and wishes. I'll come back to Phyllis in a minute. First, I want to give an illustration of how characters you play live inside you and appear when you think you're just out in the world, being you.

My next acting challenge was to be Frau Blucher in Mel Brooks's 1974 film *Young Frankenstein*. When Mel sent me the script, I don't think I read it all the way through. I don't like to read scripts, because it takes too much hard work. I'm left-handed, so I have a tendency to read things backward. From what I did read, it was obvious this was high comedy, even farce. I wanted to be funny, but I also wanted to have some reality, to be someone you wouldn't forget. I didn't know what I was going to do with the role till I got on the stage the first day.

To begin with, I'd never done a German accent, and I had no real idea what it should sound like. I went to everybody on the set, trying to find someone who knew German. Mel Brooks's mother was there, and she saw my consternation and offered to help. I couldn't have found anyone better. She knew German and led me through my initial contact with the language. In the film, I pronounce my first line, "I am Frau Blucher," very carefully because I was still a little unsure about the accent.

I then figured out how my hair should be, how I should use make-up to shape my face, and what my attitude toward the other characters should be. For me, Frau Blucher was not the kind of character to whom you apply the Stanislavsky method. She mostly sprang full grown on the set.

Being between Mel Brooks and Gene Wilder was a brand-new and vivid experience. They are two of the funniest, most off-the-wall men not only in show business but in the world. The whole shooting schedule bubbled with their humor.

I think some of my best lines are not in the picture, because Gene couldn't control his laughter when I said them. Every time I'd say a line, he'd break up, so we'd have to shoot the scene again. And again. I had a little better control than he did but the same thing would happen to me. Gene would say a line and I'd look at him with that hat he had on, at his surprised eyes, his consuming naivete, and I couldn't help but laugh. Oh, it was fun to work with the two of them.

Frau Blucher was probably the most outlandish role I have ever played. Even today I can go to my table in a restaurant and suddenly hear someone make that whinnying sound of the horses. Incidentally, there's a little joke about that, which I don't think many people know. In German the word *Blucher* means "glue," so in the film, when the horses hear the name Frau Blucher, they think they're going to be sent to the glue factory. That's why they get up on their back legs and whinny in protest.

I've even had a waiter come up to me as I've been perusing my menu and say, "You would like a little warm milk . . . Ovaltine?" Walking down the street, I've heard a voice call out, sometimes from the other side, "Yes, yes, he vas my boyfriend!" I'll look, and somebody will be giving me a big wave.

Frau Blucher got inside me, and in the months after the picture was finished, she would appear when she hadn't been sent for. She'd take over my face, my posture, and I would have to move over for her. At dinner with George one night, I felt her rise in me.

"Honey, hold on," I said.

"What's up?" George senses when a visitation might be coming.

"Zis will have to stop!" My face was now Frau Blucher's face.

"What has to stop, babe?"

"Ich bin no Babe. Ich bin Frau Blucher." I fixed him with the Frau Blucher look.

"Right, babe, er, Frau."

"Zis eating of food must end."

"Right. Foul idea. We'll quit."

"Jawohl," I murmured.

I slid back into Cloris, and we continued our dinner.

"I thought we might need an exorcism," George murmured.

Another time I played the mother superior of a Catholic order in a television film called *Dixie: Changing Habits*. Suzanne Pleshette was Dixie, a whorehouse madam who, having been convicted three times, was sent to our convent instead of being imprisoned. There I was to show her a better way of life. In one scene we were shooting, I was supposed to reveal to her the beauty in the prayer of St. Francis. When the director said, "Action," I spoke my lines.

"The prayer, Dixie, begins, 'Lord, make me an instrument of Thy peace. Where there is hatred, let me sow love; where there is injury, pardon; where there is doubt, faith . . . .'"

The director called, "Cut!"

He and Suzanne were staring at me. It wasn't me talking; the voice of one-hundred-year-old Grandma Moses was saying the lines. I'd played her in a one-woman show the year before, and it was her voice reciting the prayer. The eyes of Suzanne and the director had been stapled to me as I'd cackled out the sacred words.

"Where'd that voice come from, Cloris?" the director asked, the eeriness of the experience showing on his face.

"I have no idea," I said. I was as startled as they were.

Suzanne began to laugh and pointed knowingly at me. She had experienced that phenomenon. Finally, all three of us were in stitches at the way that antique larynx had taken over and wheezed out, "Lord, make me an instrument of Thy peace." That is the kind of schizophrenia that can go on inside you when you've played several very different women in a row.

At another point in the story, I was showing Dixie what we convent members did on our farm. I'd given her a few religious things to think about, and now I wanted her to see the benefit of growing things. I was driving a tractor, and she was standing on the flatbed trailer behind it, still dressed in her madam's fancy clothes. As we talked and I showed her where we grew the corn and the cabbages, I turned off the dirt road and into a field that had recently been plowed.

I knew very little about driving a tractor, and Suzanne knew even less about how to hang on in a flatbed trailer being dragged along behind a tractor. I didn't slow down as I made the turn, so when I hit the first row of hard dirt, Suzanne was tossed on her derriere. I didn't realize it, and I kept on driving and playing the scene, until the assistant director raced up and waved me to a stop. Suzanne tried to laugh, but she was in real pain and had to be carried to the nurse's vehicle. It turned out she was so badly bruised, she couldn't work the next day. Losing a day's shooting on a TV film is a very big deal.

I want to say a word about Suzanne. She and I were not intimate friends, but we were fellow travelers in the acting world. We knew its ins and outs. We'd run into each other at parties or at one of the networks, and we'd always have a wonderful exchange. Suzanne had her own special sparkle. Sometimes she seemed almost tough, but that was on the outside. Inside was a dear, dear person, a girl I loved. When Suzanne became seriously ill, I tried to contact her, but it was too late. She was past the point where she could respond. I miss her. I miss the color, the originality, the special way of being a woman and an actress that was hers.

All right. Back to Phyllis—a confession first. I'm always

late; I've been late all my life. My father drove me to school every day when I was little, and we would almost always arrive late. I don't know if that's when my habitual tardiness got started. It could be. I could just have adopted being late as the way you did things. But I think my lateness comes from something else.

From my earliest days, I saw myself as an artist, therefore, I should be concerned with things essential to the life of an artist. Being punctual isn't one of them. Neither is living by the rules. Since my childhood, I have disliked rules and, for the most part, have avoided them.

The day I auditioned for *The Mary Tyler Moore Show*, I arrived late, probably twenty-five to thirty minutes after the appointed hour. When the receptionist brought me to the inner office, the producers and writers and Mary were sitting in a loose semicircle. They all greeted me, Hi, Cloris. Thanks for coming. That sort of thing.

I'd heard that Jim Brooks, the cocreator of the show, thought I was a fine dramatic actress but had serious doubt that I could be the zany, self-oriented Phyllis they were looking for. So, instead of exchanging greetings with the group, I said, "Which one is Jim?" Jim Brooks pleasantly raised his hand. I walked over to him and sat on his lap and gave him a reassuring hug. That started everybody laughing. I stayed on Jim's lap for the whole interview, answering questions, being raucous, in all ways showing I could be even nuttier than the Phyllis they had in mind. The laughter was nonstop. Jim laughed harder every time I turned and gave him a sexy look. The reason I'd come was to read the part for them, we didn't bother. The role was mine.

The Mary Tyler Moore Show is the best known TV series of those I've appeared in. Though the show was on in the 1970s, nowadays people still come up to me and say, "Cloris, I grew up with you. I never missed an episode of *The Mary Tyler Moore Show*. Was that kooky Phyllis you, or did you invent her? What kind of husband was Lars? He must have been as loony as you. What did your kids think when they saw you on the show?"

The years I spent on *The Mary Tyler Moore Show* were a small lifetime, and all of us were part of a family. When creative people work together, and their respect for, and confidence in, each other grow with each performance, they develop an intimacy that is, in a way, the best expression of family.

Under the excellent leadership of our production staff, the show was perfectly organized and ran with great efficiency. Mary was always on time and ready to perform, a model for the rest of the cast. Ed Asner and Gavin Mac-Leod were equally professional; they were always punctual and always ready with their lines. That isn't to say there wasn't spontaneity and humor on the set. In between studying our revisions, we shot comments and laugh lines to each other.

Ted Knight had a tough life. He was a ventriloquist, and there was meager demand for that talent in show business. Jay, our director, mentioned more than once how difficult it was working with Ted, but that changed, and

Ted became one of the best liked members of the cast. He also became mayor of Brentwood, where we lived, and my kids always reported that he was so kind to them when they ran into him.

The person I had the most doubt about was Gavin MacLeod. I'd worked with him before, and he'd always played a menacing heavy, so I didn't know how his persona would work in a sitcom. But Gavin emerged new and splendid, he played his character with real sweetness. He conducted himself in a less bumptious way than I did—Gavin didn't sit on anybody's lap—he overcame all reservations about him doing comedy the same way I overcame Jim Brooks' reservations about me.

I never knew Jim Brooks well. But one day, while we were waiting for the set to be changed, I gave him a head-and-shoulders rub, something I do well. After it, Jim thanked me and went to his office. Later he came back on the set and sat down beside me. "I don't know what you did," he said, "but I went back into my office and burst into tears. I couldn't stop crying." It seemed my massage had released some very deep feelings. That was the closest Jim and I have ever been.

Ed Asner and I came together slowly but ended up pals. He always told me he loved me, and every once in a while, he'd grab me and whisper, "You're God's gift to man!" One day we made an agreement that I would have sex with him if he lost thirty-two pounds. Well, don't you know, he almost did it; he lost twenty-nine pounds. We both got so disoriented at what we were facing that his weight shot back up, and our assignation never happened.

Since the end of *The Mary Tyler Moore Show,* I've seen Ed occasionally. We've run into each other on television shows. Each time I've felt there was something close to hostility in his behavior. On one of these shows, with an audience of three hundred or so people, he bellowed at me, "You can't be trusted. You're absolutely untrustworthy," and his raging continued. At first, I didn't understand what was causing it.

In the years since *The Mary Tyler Moore Show,* Ed has been involved in politics, and he asked me to participate in different events. I did for a while, but I found I didn't always agree with his positions on things, and tending to be outspoken myself, I thought it better to leave off doing them.

I concluded later that his antipathy toward me had grown out of my unwillingness to associate myself with his political activities. But in speaking to his son one evening, I realized it wasn't politics. He was unhappy that I had talked in public about the terms we'd agreed on for a sexual encounter and why that encounter didn't happen. I thought it was funny, and I still do, but if Ed feels otherwise and he happens to read this far in this book, I want him to know that if I hurt him I am deeply sorry, and I love him just as much as I did when we were on the show. And, if he still thinks he can "make the weight," we might put that sumo match together again.

On Mondays we gathered to read the script. The next two days we'd stage the show, and late on Wednesday Jim Brooks and Allan Burns, the show's other cocreator, would watch a run-through. After it they'd give us suggestions; Jim's were especially creative, fresh, and unexpected.

From then on, right up to the filming on Friday afternoon, when we did two performances in front of audiences, we were constantly fed new revisions. So often as we were filming I'd be tossing away my revised script with my left hand as I was opening the door with my right to enter the set, and spout the lines I'd just thrown away.

Mary didn't need a lot of rehearsal, but Valerie Harper and I were from the stage, and rehearsal was essential to us, so we'd meet at lunch. We didn't actually rehearse as we ate, that is, we didn't run lines. We discussed, swapped ideas, and decided how we'd handle a scene. Then we'd get in front of the cameras and make magic. My character, Phyllis, as I said, had a runaway ego. She did as she liked and didn't withhold her opinions, whether they were asked for or not. From the beginning, Phyllis and I were doppelgängers: I behaved off camera much as I did in front of the camera. Being late was my most pronounced behavioral "diversion," but it wasn't the only one. What crinkled the cast and crew more than my tardiness was my disregard for the rules. To me, it wasn't being disobedient, I was an artist living an artist's life, and I didn't have to obey rules created by others. I was being Peck's bad boy. *Peck's Bad Boy* is the self-explanatory title of a movie I'd seen when I was a child.

During the show, I often did television interviews. One night I was on *The Tonight Show Starring Johnny Carson* . . . Let me go back a step. The month before the Johnny Carson appearance, I had an interview in my trailer on the set of *The Mary Tyler Moore Show*. Following my directions, my assistant had made a tasty lunch for the female interviewer and me. The interviewer was interested in how I'd come to create the dish and what my views were on diet and nutrition. I said I wished that people who were gaining too much weight could sample what we were having for lunch, because it was tasty but not fattening.

The article was published, and it included a description of our lunch and my saying how desirable this approach to cooking would be for people who needed to lose weight, fat people. During my interview with Johnny Carson, he asked me about the article and what its main point was. Typical of me, I said what jumped into my mind, that there were too many overweight people walking around and that we should have "fat catchers" to bring them in for treatment. Johnny was not often speechless, but at that moment I saw it in his eyes: he'd been hit by a Taser.

This was twenty years before concerns about obesity in America had crystallized, so my remarks caused a considerable stir. The network got hundreds of letters, and so did I. One of my closest friends said that I should get security around the house, because there were some very irate overweight people who might want to do me harm. The irony is that today I am one of those people who should be rounded up by a fat catcher. I've gained too much weight, but I'm going to attack the problem, and by the time you get to this page in the book, I'll be my sylphlike self again.

Back to being Peck's bad boy. At the same time my undisciplined behavior at work was getting attention, my personal life was in chaos. I was having the house worked on, and there were literally eighteen workmen there every day, and they needed their questions answered. George and I were separating, my daughter, Dinah, was five years old and needed me, and my son Bryan was in New York, using drugs—he'd call and say someone had stolen his coat or some other such improbable story, and I would send him money. I had not learned that any money I sent him, whatever the alleged reason, would be used to buy drugs.

I don't offer my personal life as an excuse for my behavior, because I was the one in control of my life. It was I who was late, I who created the chaos at home. I've asked myself if this was compulsive behavior or if I had a choice. Could I have done my work on the show professionally, been on time and observed the rules, and conducted my personal life in a responsible way? I'm not sure. I really don't know if I could have chosen to act differently then.

But things began to change. Valerie Harper was the reason. She was always my defender; she supported me unequivocally and at all times. She once told me, "We all ought to bow down to you, get down on our hands and knees, because you're the only one who's doing it right." She called me her girlfriend. No one had called me that before. I was terribly moved by her unflagging support. It brought a change in me.

The need to be late and behave erratically began to fade. Because of Valerie's positive picture of me, I was able to let go of the life mode I had adopted. One day I said it out loud. I was in the make-up chair. Ben Nye was putting on my eyeliner, and I said, "It's going to be different, Ben. I'm going to be different. I just want you to know that." He seemed to grasp what I was saying. He smiled, and from that moment on, his attitude toward me was different. Life was different. I'd been released. I didn't have to be Peck's bad boy anymore. I could if I wanted to, but I didn't have to.

At the end of the last show, we had a party, with food and drinks, an all-out festivity. Everyone talked and took pictures, said good-bye, we signed our autographs for each other. We were like a sorority, a fraternity. We belonged to each other. When we ran into each other later on, even though time had passed by, we were just as familiar. "Hi. Well, you look old," one might say. "Yeah, you look old, too," the other would reply. Then we'd both laugh.

So the fervent years on *The Mary Tyler Moore Show*—the portraying of dear, unbridled Phyllis and the care and support of Valerie Harper—brought a welcome and significant reward.

The success of *The Mary Tyler Moore Show* impelled the producers to create a spin-off called *Phyllis*, in which I starred. It lasted two wonderful years (1975–1977). I loved doing the show, and I loved every single cast member.

The show was a hit from the beginning, and the series pilot was hilarious. In that first episode, my character, Phyllis, goes to an employment agency and is interviewed by Doris Roberts. She asks me what skills I possess. I inform her that one of my major talents is knowing which wine goes best with every sort of meal. As she continues to question me, she suddenly realizes that she wants that job. So right there, in the middle of the interview, she puts down her pen, opens the bottom desk door, grabs her purse, and rushes out to get the job herself—while I sit waiting.

One thing was missing in the show—a person for me to

bump against, to compete with, the way I did with Rhoda on *The Mary Tyler Moore Show*. Valerie Harper and I were perfect adversaries on the MTM landscape; each was totally intolerant of the other's views, and that made great comedy.

There were other holes in *Phyllis*. In the two-year period that the show aired, three members of the cast died. In 1975, when we were starting our fourth episode, Barbara Colby was murdered. She was only thirty-five years old and had appeared with me in one of my best TV films, *A Brand New Life*. She and a friend were shot inside a parking area; Barbara died instantly.

In December 1976, Judith Lowry, who played eighty-six-year-old Mother Dexter, died right after the episode in which she married her ninety-two-year-old boyfriend, Arthur, played by Burt Mustin. Two months later Burt Mustin was gathered. It was this combination of things that, I think, ended our run in 1977.

In 1986 Charlotte Rae had reached her endpoint in the TV series *The Facts of Life*. The girls with whom she had started the show had by then grown up quite a bit, and Charlotte wasn't as comfortable with the new issues she faced as she had been with the old. I was approached by the producers of the show to replace Charlotte. I hadn't seen the show, and my initial reaction was not immediately positive. However, after watching the show and considering what I could do with the role, I said yes.

I hadn't seen Charlotte in years, so we had a sentimental reunion. She came up with my character's first name by combining her sisters' names, Beverly and Ann. My then manager, Steve Vail, and I decided to make separate lists of possible last names. The next day we talked on the phone and alternated reading the names on each of our lists. We each had ten names. We didn't find one we both liked until near the end, when I said, "Stickle," and, a huge surprise to both of us, he said, "Stickle." We were astonished that we had both chosen such an unusual name. That's how we knew it was the right one. So Stickle it was.

I enjoyed my time on *The Facts of Life*. Each episode was a new kind of fun as we solved the girls' problems. The four of us really did become a family. The girls are grown up now and scattered around the country, but the joy we had in working together comes back with all its original fervor every time I run into one of them.

A Bit of History

In preparation for this book, I asked for a list of the Broadway productions, films, and television shows in which I've appeared. It's in front of me now, and as my eyes run down the columns, even I am surprised at the numbers.

> BROADWAY PLAYS: 11
> FILMS: 57
> TELEVISION SHOWS: 137

My mind flicks back over the different roles; different costumes; different eras in history; the Broadway openings; the world premieres; the TV series; the tearful departures when they were over; the faces that were part of those productions, some instantly familiar, some brought back from the outer fringes of memory, many having passed on. I recall the care we took of each other, the way we worked to create the best possible performance.

My thoughts come to rest on my one-woman show about Grandma Moses. She began painting late in life and became famous for her "primitive art." In the first act, I portrayed her as what she was then, a woman in her early sixties, living on her farm, starting to paint, and having no idea that she would become famous. And she certainly didn't know she was going to live for another forty odd years.

At the opening of the second act, I came onstage when she was about to leave for Washington, D.C., where she was going to be honored by the president of the United States on her hundredth birthday. The curtain rose on the set of her living room; no one was there. After a moment I entered and took a measured walk across the front of the set to pick up the hat and gloves I was going to wear in Washington. I walked slowly, the years having reduced my speed. My lower jaw was protruding and making contact in a chewing motion with my upper teeth.

The audience was silent at first, then, as I continued across the stage, there were gasps. It was a holy moment for me, one of my best as an actress. I could hear, I could feel, the audience seeing me, experiencing me, as this hundred-year-old woman.

It came from inside me. I hadn't studied the physiology of old age. I had sat alone and imagined how the act of walking would feel when I was a hundred years old, how my capacity to proceed in a straight line would have weakened, how my bones and ligaments would have dried and thinned after such long use.

I want to portray Grandma Moses again. Creating the character this time will be a different challenge, I'll be ten years nearer to a hundred myself. Recreating Grandma Moses in her early sixties, her quick laughter, her springy step, her farm woman's vitality, will be the task next time.

Acting With Criminal Intent

I have been guilty of theft more times than I can remember. I have stolen from my children.

That's not a confession. I say it with pride because to excel, to produce memorable characterizations, actors have to be good thieves. We actors must be on the alert to see, to inhale, the instant when someone is hysterical or sublimely pleased or inconsolably grief stricken or enjoying her fried chicken. These moments are the currency of good acting. If you want the audience to sigh, to hope, to regret, maybe even to wish to die, then recall a time when you were in the middle of that reality. It is there in the tumble of your experiences.

In a Western TV series called *Stoney Burke*, I played a girl who was mostly a boy. She'd grown up among wranglers, and she knew everything about shoeing horses and mucking stalls and nothing about being female. In one scene I was walking by the corral with one of the wranglers, and he said something that was distinctly related to my being an appealing young girl. The girl I was playing didn't know how to react. Feelings she'd never known suddenly pulsed through her, she felt gushy and embarrassed. How would I bring all that into my reaction?

I thought back to when my son Bryan was nine years old. He loved go-karts and was expert with them. One day one of the girls who'd come with us to the track watched him win a race and afterward told him how marvelously he'd driven, how fearless he'd seemed. Love was shining in her eyes. This was all new for Bryan. Sex and the female gender hit him in the face like a lemon meringue pie. His features went askew, he leered, he made a snorting sound, he looked away, he looked at me, and finally, with great difficulty, he looked at her. It was a moment out of time, Adam and Eve realizing they were different from what they'd thought, that they were female and male, man and woman, and, oh my, what a different world theirs would be from then on.

In the part of my soul where the golden memories lie is that one when the maleness in Bryan was stirred for the first time. As I played that girl in *Stoney Burke*, I closed my eyes, not only to see that moment with Bryan again, but to bring it inside me. Using the emotions I'd stolen from Bryan, I created one of the most live and most real moments I have ever put on film. Indeed, it was one of the most tender moments I have ever experienced.

The director and members of the crew told me afterward how touched they'd been as they'd looked on, how they'd both laughed and cried. I thanked them as inwardly I felt the joy of stealing that moment from my son. I wished he'd been there to tell me if I got it right.

Technical Matters

Film will soon disappear as the medium in which motion pictures are made. In the visible future, everything will be shot, stored, and edited digitally. It's essential for actors to be familiar with the changing technical landscape. Sometimes actors feel they're the creative part of the process and don't need to know about the technical gizmos.

That was never true. Even in silent films actors learned how they were lighted, how they were framed, and which lens was on the camera. On the night I won my Oscar, which was the same night that Charlie Chaplin won his Lifetime Achievement Award, at the party afterward, he told me how moved he was to have the award and how it took him back to when his career began.

He started working in pantomime companies and music halls, and he gained some success as an actor. When he got to Hollywood and started applying for acting jobs there, he realized he was in a new world, with a whole new way to tell stories and act in them. Chaplin invaded that new world, learned all its technicalities, then began adding his own tools, tricks, and methods. Against the background of the Oscar party, it was exhilarating to hear him tell of his beginnings, and it enlarged my perspective.

As the technologies in television and movie making expand, I'm not as determined as I should be to keep up with the new demands and new tools. I tend to be willful, and I'm easily bored these days, so don't be like me. Be like young Charlie Chaplin feasting on the new things he could learn, the new ways he could use his talent.

Actors and the Other Arts

Actors have two major tools to use, their voice and their body. To ply their trade successfully, they should have maximum control and extract maximum use from these tools. The voice should be able to produce any effect, from loudness and softness to dark tones, light tones, breathiness, and bombast. I studied singing from the time I was seven, and still today the scales and vocalizing help me in whatever performance I'm creating, comedy, melodrama, or tragedy.

Dance is an excellent way to develop both fluidity and control of the body. I began studying ballet at seven, too, and it's hard for me to estimate how many times and in how many different ways I've used my experience with ballet. Even now, while I'm writing this book, I'm rehearsing every day for *Dancing with the Stars*. I'll say what that's been like later on.

One instance where my dance training came into play was in creating zany Phyllis on *The Mary Tyler Moore Show*. The flouncy way I entered Mary's living room, the pirouettes I used to turn away from and show my diffidence to Rhoda, the arm movement Phyllis used to bring attention to herself and to make clear she was no ordinary nine-to-five housewife were all rooted in my dance training.

It doesn't have to be ballet. Today's dances are entertaining and demanding. The important thing is that dance gives an actress energy and control of her body and more ways to illustrate the person she's portraying.

The other arts, painting, sculpture, music, can be fountains of inspiration, too. Study a portrait by Rembrandt van Rijn or Diego Velázquez or Frans Hals. Really study it. See the massive amount of information and emotion the artist gives you about his subject.

One of Michelangelo's most famous sculptures depicts Moses after he's had his conversation with God and been given the Ten Commandments. He's sitting on a throne-like chair, and the somber look on his face says he's uncertain how to tell his people what he's just experienced. It's a complex, monumental piece of work, the folds of the toga, the veins in the leg, the expression in the eyes, it's almost incomprehensible how all that could be carved out of one giant piece of marble.

There is a crack in the left knee, and the story is that Michelangelo, at eighty-three years old, feeling he'd finished the work, stepped back to appraise it. He was struck dumb, awed at the ability God had given him to rescue characters from a cold slab of marble and give them life. The statue seemed so lifelike that he stepped forward and hit the knee with his chisel and said, "Speak!" That strike to the knee produced the famous crack. We actors should attempt to be as amazed at the characters we create as Michelangelo was by those he brought to life.

Did you ever notice how before their events, swimmers and boxers often have a device in their ears and nod their heads or sway to the music that's coming out of it? Depending on what music they've chosen, they are hearing something soothing or a summons to courage, whatever music they want to affect them. I am always immersed in music. Either I'm playing it or listening to it, and I'm always being affected by it. When I'm creating a character, I think of what music fits her, what she would like to listen to, what emotional responses she would have. It's another dimension in knowing the person you want to portray.

Hemingway, in describing sharks, said the mako is not the biggest shark, but "the mako feeds on everything in the ocean." I say actors should be mako sharks. Only they shouldn't restrict their consumption to the ocean. They should feed on everything and everybody in the world.

Mothers

I've played a rainbow of female parents. I've arched over the lives of: Meryl Streep. Diane Keaton. Meg Ryan. Téa Leoni. Ron Howard. Ellen DeGeneres. Jeff Goldblum. Donald Sutherland. Lisa Kudrow. Jane Kaczmarek. Howie Mandel. John Larroquette. Sissy Spacek. Cybill Shepherd. And forty others.

With each, I was a specific part of a specific family. I loathe clichés, and I was a sentinel against becoming a generic mother who's the same every time you see her. Offscreen, I and whoever was my child often stayed in our roles and talked as if we were actually mother and daughter or mother and son; we exchanged worries, thoughts, and aspirations, and we counseled each other about our lives.

As to how I characterize the different mothers, I've been "kindly and understanding" (*Lassie*), "alcoholic" (*Spanglish*), "overbearing and racially insensitive" (*Malcolm in the Middle*), and "sexy" (*The Longest Yard*). In fact, as a mother, I have worn almost every imaginable personality.

Here's a partial list of my maternal endeavors.

Meryl Streep; *Music of the Heart* (1999)

Let me say first that I think Meryl is the best actress working today. I played her mother in *Music of the Heart.*

One evening on the way home, I ran into Mindy Cohn, who'd played one of the girls in the TV series *The Facts of Life* with me. Mindy asked if I could get Meryl's autograph for her. I said I thought there'd be no problem, I would ask.

Meryl was gracious, she said she'd be happy to sign a picture for Mindy. But she never did. The whole shooting schedule went by, we wrapped after the last take, and I realized I didn't have the autograph. So I knocked on Meryl's trailer door. Her assistant answered and ushered me in. Meryl was in a dressing gown, smoking, and right there she signed a picture for Mindy.

Then she asked, "Would you like one, Cloris?"

I said, "Oh, thanks. Yes, I would." I thought she'd write something like "From one fantastic actress to another, it was great working together." Instead, she wrote, "Cloris, you were unforgivably skinny through the whole picture. Love, Meryl."

That is Meryl. So often in her film roles, she is the picture of refinement, and she truly is a refined woman, but off the set, this almost locker-room humor, exists, too. When I say I consider Meryl the best actress working today, it's because of the diversity of roles she's played and the diligent, imaginative way she goes about creating her characters. If she has to have an accent, she will, through her own research process, produce it faultlessly. But she doesn't just do a good accent. The person behind that accent, whose roots are in a different culture, a different country, is what she creates so tellingly. Anyone pursuing acting today would do well to study not only Meryl's body of work but the dignity with which she has conducted her life and her career.

Diane Keaton, Meg Ryan, and Lisa Kudrow; *Hanging Up* (2000)

I'm taking credit for being the mother of all three of them, since that was the situation in the film, but in fact, I had a scene with only one of my children, Meg Ryan. This was long before Meg became the charming, grown-up star who radiates zest in so many excellent films. This was when she had just left childhood behind.

I don't have many sharp memories from making that film. What stands out most is that Diane Keaton also directed it. As the director, she did bizarre things. When we filmed my scene, first we shot the master angle. Then, when it came to my close-up, Diane gave Meg completely different lines from those in the script to read to me off camera. This was a substantial breach of professional comportment: you don't, in the middle of shooting a scene, give one actor completely different lines to say to another actor. Actors are obliged to come to the set knowing their lines. I've skidded around orthodoxy sometimes, but I have always come to the set knowing my lines.

The only explanation for Diane's behavior I could imagine was that as a first-time director, she just simply didn't know what directing a picture entailed. Thinking as kindly as I could, I imagined she wanted, for some reason, to provoke a different reaction from the one I'd had in the master angle, but she didn't talk with me about it. It was a little secret she kept to herself, hardly a sensible way to get something out of an actress.

Donald Sutherland; *Beerfest* (2006)

When you're playing someone's mother in a film, things can be very different from what you expected. In *Beerfest* I played Donald's mother, but we never once saw each other. We never even shook hands. The only time we were in a scene together was at a service in church after he had died. He, that is, the character he was playing, had made a DVD, which he wanted those he had left behind to view at this memorial service. Nothing in the script gave any indication about what sort of relationship we'd had as mother and son.

So while we were all watching the DVD in the church, it seemed to me the only thing I could do was be the cliché mother, sad and tearful. If there's anything I truly dislike in acting—well, in life, too—it's clichés, but I played the scene with that synthetic emotion. The picture is raucous, and I guess the scene works acceptably, but I don't want anyone to tell me it's one of my all-time best performances.

Téa Leoni; *Spanglish* (2004)

I hadn't worked with Jim Brooks since *The Mary Tyler Moore Show*. He'd become very successful with his film, *Terms of Endearment*, and he'd gone on from there. During those years on MTM, I came to have great respect for both Jim's talent and his hard work. No matter how late it got or how many rewrites there had been, Jim wouldn't settle till he felt he'd got the script right.

I'd heard how hard and long he'd worked on the screenplay of *Spanglish* and I felt nothing less than honored when he asked me to be part of it. I replaced Anne Bancroft, who'd become ill, and that made something of a ripple in the company. Anne was loved by everyone connected to the project, so the person who now stood in her place would not find a flower-strewn path. I understood. I knew it wasn't personal, and I'd been through similar situations. The company was friendly enough. There were no dark looks, nothing like that, just a sense of loss that Anne was gone.

One person helped most. I was playing Téa Leoni's mother, and from the first day, Téa was cordial, supportive, sensitive about the situation and wonderful to work with. She removed any shred of discomfort I might have felt. She seemed to me the consummate actress and woman.

The woman I played was an alcoholic. I'd never been much of a drinker, so I had some learning to do. I didn't do detailed research. I didn't go to AA meetings, I didn't hang out at Flanagan's Bar down the street, and I didn't interrogate women I knew who were alcoholic. Rather I observed those women, picked up their characteristics, and stored them. Principally, I observed my relationship with the other actors, watched how they reacted to me, especially my daughter. Then, using what I'd seen in alcoholic women and taking Jim's direction, I shaped my performance.

When filming was over, I told Jim Brooks that at the beginning, I'd felt I needed training in portraying an alcoholic, so I'd started drinking. I'd been bingeing every day. It had been a heavy grind, I said, but I thought things were going to work out well, because he was pleased with my performance, and that was the most important thing. Also, things were now going pretty well in my personal life. I was three weeks into rehab, and I was starting to sleep without convulsions, and my kids were talking to me again. So life was good. We chuckled.

Cybill Shepherd; *Daisy Miller* (1974)

This opulent period picture, directed by Peter Bogdanovich, in which I played Cybill Shepherd's mother, was shot in Rome.

During the filming, a classic Hollywood backstage drama was going on: the star and the director were having a passionate affair. I can't say their relationship had any negative effect on the production. In fact, it added a bloom to everything. The paparazzi were everywhere, and Peter and Cybill fairly glowed when they looked at each other.

As for my own role, two things puzzled me. First, I was kind of little, and Cybill was kind of big. Secondly, I was married to a very rich man. I could not explain to myself how I'd ended up with this large, beautiful daughter and how I'd come to be married to a rich guy. So I pretended to myself that I was a little brown duck, and somehow I'd laid a great big white egg, which turned out to be Cybill. As for my marriage, I felt that my husband didn't know I was a little brown duck. Instead, he saw a large, regal woman. That's how I played my scenes with him.

Ellen DeGeneres; *The Ellen Show* (2001–2002)

Playing Ellen's mother on *The Ellen Show* was fun. We both like to improvise and be a little crazy on the set. One day during rehearsal, I said to Ellen, "Sometimes I can go on too much or too long or, you know, sort of get out of hand. If I do, I want you to remember the solution George uses. When I'm taking over a room, talking fast and eating other people's food and generally being, well, me, he'll call out, 'Babe . . .' I'll look over, and he'll raise both hands like this—and make the sound of air going out of a balloon. I'll get the picture and slow down."

The premise of the TV series was that Ellen had left her life in the city and had come back home, to her rural roots, to live with me, her mother. It was always pleasant and pastoral. We never discussed the actualities, that she was a lesbian and that that fact could cause a stir in our little tucked-away valley. We just played the scenes as mother and daughter, and the most that appeared in the show was the occasional hint that she was not going to date some of the guys she had known in high school. Ellen is the genuine article, a real pro. You're as much at home with her in a sitcom as when you're being interviewed on her talk show.

Jane Kaczmarek; *Malcolm in the Middle* (2001–2006)

I had to do the most embarrassing things playing Jane's mother in the TV series *Malcolm in the Middle*. The producers wanted me to have an accent. I said, "Fine. Which one?" They told me not to do the accent of a specific country, make one up. That was because some of what I said and did was outrageous and bordered on the reprehensible. They didn't want anyone to be offended. So I went into my linguistic kitchen and cooked up a goulash, which, everyone tells me, sounded real. My real success was that this accent couldn't be attributed to any nation or race. People sometimes come up to me and ask what accent I used in *Malcolm in the Middle*.

"My grandmother sort of talks the way you do, and she's from Romania. Is that a Romanian accent?"

"Ah," I'll say, "close but no cigar. The way I talk comes from my own life. I spent time in Romania, but that was after I'd lived in Cuba and Israel and Georgia. But you've got a good ear. There is a whisper of Romanian in there."

I did do some hilarious but outrageous things on the show. When I came to visit Jane and her family, I wouldn't speak to her son's wife, because she was Korean. When the wife greeted me, I didn't acknowledge her. I didn't even look at her. I said to Jane, "Tell the help not to talk to me," and I went on smoking imperiously. If I had been German or Hungarian or something recognizable, people would have called in and said, "You're making us look like impolite idiots. We're going to boycott your show." I hope my generic accent continues to be successful, and no one is offended by my character. She isn't me. I'm nothing like that, but people like her do exist.

Shirley Temple; *Shirley Temple Theatre* (1960)

There's not a lot to say about playing Shirley's mother. It was a long time ago, and the shooting schedule was short. The memory that stands out is this. We were working on a soundstage at Twentieth Century-Fox studio, and I needed to make an important phone call. This was long before cell phones. I couldn't locate a phone. I knew there had to be one, but where was it?

I turned to Shirley and said, "Shirley, you must know where there's a phone. You worked at Twentieth your whole early life. Where is it?"

She said, "I don't know. I was only three feet tall then. I couldn't even reach a phone."

Of all the mother roles I've played, these next two affected me the most.

Ron Howard, Sissy Spacek;
The Migrants (1974)

This television film is based on a Tennessee Williams story. It's about a family of nomadic farmworkers who travel from Florida to New England, picking beans, tomatoes, and peppers. They're paid by the bushel. It's a life of desperate poverty. I played the mother, who is struggling to keep her family together and who will not lose hope that her son will find a better life somewhere. "Don't be less than you can be," I say to him. "Don't be less than your dream. That's what I want from you."

The feelings I had during filming didn't leave me when the day was over; the awful burden of having to save my children was real to me every minute. Still today I'm left with emotions I can't handle from playing that role.

I was nominated for an Emmy for *The Migrants*. On the night of the awards, I came home with two grocery bags. I put them down in the kitchen and went into my bedroom and turned on the TV. As soon as the picture came on, I saw a clip of Cicely Tyson in *The Autobiography of Miss Jane Pittman*. She was walking to the "Whites Only" drinking fountain. She was mesmerizing. I said, "Bye-bye, Emmy." I knew she'd win it, and she did. I walked back into the kitchen and put the groceries away.

I don't want to seem immodest, but I'd like to include parts of two reviews I received for *The Migrants*.

The New York Times

"Cloris Leachman, as the Elmer's Glue-All that holds this family together through the inauspicious birth of her grandchild, the death by tuberculosis of her son-in-law, the ambition to be gone of her son, the mute endurance of her husband, is splendid. She is such a good actress that she has the courage to appear ugly when the role demands it. Indeed, she disappears into the role; we are never conscious of any acting . . . Her climactic scene in *The Migrants* could have been a tantrum or, more inflationary, a snake-pit showstopper, madness rampant. As she plays it, [her] character is like an arched bow: the string snaps, the bow breaks. Mend the bow."

Variety

"The portrayal by Cloris Leachman in *The Migrants,* surely one of the best in an already distinguished list, gives her a depth and dimension one encounters rarely on stage and practically never on television."

The Woman Who Willed a Miracle (1983)

I put this one last because I feel it is not only the best mother role I played, it is the best acting I've ever done. To be precise, I was the foster mother, not the actual mother, of my son in this television film based on a true story.

CLORIS

I played May Lemke, a middle-aged nurse with grown children, who, along with her husband, takes in as a foster child an abandoned baby boy. The boy, whom they call Leslie, is blind, severely retarded, and suffers from cerebral palsy. I, as May, patiently, enthusiastically and unflaggingly teach Leslie how to eat, walk, and talk.

Handicapped as he is, the boy is able to do very little, but I am resolved to help him. I surround him with positive energy, chuckling and cajoling, singing and dancing, and praising him. One day Leslie shows an interest in music. It's there briefly, then it seems to languish, until suddenly, when he is a teenager, he sits down at the piano one day and plays a classical piece perfectly all the way through. It turns out he has genius in this area. Blue skies open for Leslie and me; neither of us has ever known a joy to compare with this. Doctors say the constant love and support May gave Leslie allowed that huge talent inside him to flower.

When I played this role, I didn't feel like an actress going to work every day. I wasn't an actress. I was May Lemke, and as this abandoned baby boy and I traveled the road of life, I made sure he would, every minute of every day, feel my devotion, my will to work a miracle, which was that he would have a good life in spite of his palsy, his retardation.

Again, I don't want to overstep the bounds of good taste, but I would like to share two of the reviews.

The New York Times

"[Miss Leachman's] Mrs. Lemke is a woman of towering stubbornness, of almost fanatical dedication. At the same time, she is an unfailing source of love . . . Miss Leachman reaches for and achieves an intensity that is virtually irresistible. She becomes a whirlwind, sweeping everyone and everything along with her."

Miami Herald

"To say Leachman is versatile does not do her justice, because each of her characters is a living, breathing, individual creation made memorable by her ability to dig inside, to come up with just the right tone and detail to show how each of them ticks. She does this once again as the indomitable May Lemke."

Props

Now to more mundane matters. We've talked about costumes and wardrobe, and I described the emphasis Elia Kazan put on having the right props and using them tellingly. When I undertake a role, right away I begin to think about the props I could use.

What are props? We ought to take a second to be specific about them. Props are anything you touch, sit on, hold in your hand, use for "business" onstage. On a hot afternoon I might have a fan. If it's a spring morning, I might carry a rose. At another time it might be useful to have a drink in my hand, or I might be pulling on my gloves. There are all kinds of prop choices for an actor to make. The way you use a prop, how you relate to it, can sometimes be the most riveting part of a scene. Props tell who a character is and help animate the scene.

Here's another acting trick that can be useful. It has nothing to do with props, but I just thought of it, so I'll put it in here. When you have to cry in a scene, instead of trying to work up tears, try *not* to cry. It will be more arresting to an audience and will produce a more dramatic effect. This method also works with laughter: when you're supposed to laugh, try not to laugh. You'll find the effect is more compelling, and that it makes the audience laugh.

You thought that was all? Not quite. There's one more thing. Risk. For me, it's important to take risks. I don't look for safety in my performance. My advice is if an idea comes, give it room. Give it a voice. If it fails, get up off your behind and try another one.

You need courage to take risks, and courage is something not generally associated with acting. For me, it's a crucial element. My definition of courage? If you know what the result will be if you do something, it doesn't take courage to do it. If you don't know what the result of an action might be, and it could be unpleasant or frightening, and you go ahead with that action, you've exhibited courage.

A Friend Becomes Ill

I thought the trail of my autobiography would lead only through the past. But the present has shouldered its way in. Not long ago, it was discovered that Teddy Kennedy has a fierce and fast-growing brain tumor. He has since undergone a surgical procedure, and now the melancholy chemotherapy protocol takes over. There is hope that Teddy, if he doesn't make a full recovery, will at least have a prolonged life. But the heartless history of this malady doesn't give much reason for hope.

As I study the latest bulletins about Teddy and the media coverage of his appearance in the Senate to vote on the Medicare bill, thoughts of sunny days with the Kennedys come back to me. In 1964 I was in New York, doing a television show with Peter Falk, when Sargent Shriver called. Sarge was director of the Peace Corps and President Kennedy's brother-in-law. He's been married all these years to Eunice Kennedy. He was calling to invite me to the Kennedy compound at Hyannis Port for the Fourth of July weekend. George was in Rome and my mother was taking care of the children back in LA., so I thought that it would be fun.

The Kennedy plane, the *Caroline,* a DC-3 named for the president and Jackie's daughter, would touch down in New York and pick me up, Sarge said. Shortly after, he called back and asked if I would mind coming down to Washington. It would be a lot easier for everybody if I could. I said, "Sure," so the next morning I got up at 6:30 and took a plane down to Washington. The *Caroline* arrived just after I did, and I met all the Kennedy children and the nurse and the pilot, and we all climbed aboard. We were a buoyant lot: the inside of the plane was jumping with ex-citement. But my excitement was short-lived. Right after takeoff, we hit a series of air pockets that turned the plane sideways and dropped us straight down. That made me sick, and I had to run into the little bathroom. And when I say little, I mean teeny. You couldn't stand up in it, and I'm only five feet four. Fortunately, it wasn't a long trip, and my brightness returned by the time we arrived at Hyannis Port.

We went immediately to visit the patriarch of the Kennedy family, Joe Kennedy. Around us as we left the airport was a full police escort, with motorcycle cops in front and alongside us, flashing red and blue lights. The vehicle we rode in had flags on the front fenders.

When we were all seated in the living room, Joe Ken-nedy was brought in, in his wheelchair. We greeted him ef-fusively. The children had gifts for him, a picture they'd made or a poem they'd written. He looked lovingly at each child and each gift, but it was plain that the flame of life in him was burning low. We didn't want to stay any longer than was wise, so soon we all kissed him and said our good-byes.

From there we went to the Shrivers' house. The year before, not long before he was killed in Texas, President Kennedy had stayed there. My room was lovely. It had a four-poster bed. At one end of the room, there was a small staircase that led down to a little sunroom. There was another bed in there, and I learned that that was probably where Eunice would sleep. Sarge had the big bed in which President Kennedy had slept.

Quickly, we all got ready to go water-skiing. Eunice drove the boat and Dick Goodwin, who wrote many of President Kennedy's speeches, came aboard with us. Goodwin was keen to try his hand at the sport. He got in the water, behind the boat, and when he signaled that he was ready, Eunice pushed the throttles forward. Goodwin couldn't pull himself even an inch above the surface of the water, and seawater was going up his nose as he was towed along at twenty miles an hour. It appeared that he did not know he had to let go of the line in order to get his nostrils back to normal size. With everyone waving at him, finally he released the line.

Eunice was patient. She circled around and came in close to Goodwin so he could grab the line again. He nodded that he was ready, and Eunice pushed the throttles forward again. This time Goodwin went the opposite way;

he gave a powerhouse yank on the line, and that jerked him up so high that he was horizontal to the water. Our eyes popped. He held that position for about a three count then he let go of the line and went into the water like a spear.

Again and again, almost exactly at five-minute intervals, the operation was repeated. Thirty minutes later, we were still waiting for Goodwin to do whatever he had to do to get upright. Eunice showed biblical patience, and finally, Goodwin did get up on the skis—but not for long. Almost immediately he crossed the wake of the boat, and that sent him into the most glorious pratfall of the day.

We returned to the house to prepare for lunch. All I had to wear was a blue muumuu I'd bought in Hawaii fifteen years earlier. My hair had been bleached white for a role I had played on television the week before, and right after that, I had dyed it brown for the Peter Falk show, so at this point, it was a color for which there is no accurate name. For lunch, I put a scarf around my head to cover my hair, and the scarf, of course, didn't at all match the faded flowered muumuu.

While the adults and the kids were playing happily, suddenly Jackie Kennedy walked in. It was a regal entrance. She was beautifully dressed in something light and sunny, and her hair was soft and natural and lovely. I felt like a ghoul as I compared her wardrobe and hairdo to mine and I immediately skulked behind the taller kids. Then something happened out on the lawn, and everybody left the room. Except Jackie and me. We were suddenly alone in this now silent place. I have to do a bit of filling in here.

Six months before, George had been in New York with Marlon Brando. The day he was to arrive back in Los Angeles, I hadn't heard from him, so late at night, I called the airport and asked when the last plane was due in from New York. They said, "Three in the morning." I waited till 3:00 a.m., and still there was no word from George, so I turned on the news and climbed into bed. It was as if the newscaster was talking to me personally. "Tonight in Washington," he said, "Jackie Kennedy had her first night out since the president was assassinated. She and her sister, Princess Lee Radziwill, dined with Marlon Brando and George Englund at one of Washington's toniest restaurants, the Jockey Club. Mrs. Kennedy, it was reported, has lost none of her radiance."

I said to the TV, "Thank you very much and bye-bye." I switched it off and went to sleep.

So, when I was suddenly alone in this sunny parlor with Jackie Kennedy, there were a couple of things I was faintly interested in knowing. Who was whose date that evening at the Jockey Club? Was she with Marlon, and was Lee with George, or was it the other way around? What did they do after dinner? Anything . . . intimate? Somehow I couldn't find a can opener to pry the subjects open. So there we were, the most famous woman in the world and me, silent and looking at each other. My mouth started to move, but the words I uttered had no connection to anything I was thinking, and I wasn't actually thinking about anything. Except that night the four of them had spent together.

I got on the subject of a wonderful children's book I'd read. "You should get it for John," I told her. (Jackie had admonished everyone not to call her son John-John. "His name is John," she would say emphatically.) I was talking fast and running out of backup topics of conversation when, blessedly, lunch was called. That interlude with Jackie was—I'm not sure how to describe it—odd, awkward, wonderful. I'd love to know what her thoughts were underneath our superficial chatter.

Sarge and Eunice had heard that I favored vegetables, so they'd had a broccoli-and-cheese casserole prepared for lunch. I was aglow; the Kennedy chef had made an item just for me. When it arrived at the table, my face fell. It was dreadfully overcooked, and I'd have needed a machete to hack through the crust. I didn't know what to say. I mean, what do you say when you're lunching at the Kennedy compound, you're the honored guest, and something like that is set in front of you? I parted my lips in a wan smile, pulled the dish close to me, and draped my napkin halfway over it, indicating I'd get to it a little bit later.

Next, clams were served. Sarge had gone to his favorite place to get them. I don't eat clams. I can't. I couldn't get a clam down if I was threatened with waterboarding. I thought to myself, *Nice going, Cloris. You want the entire Kennedy family to know that the best of what they eat is not acceptable to you.* Not knowing what face to put on, I started talking. The quiet hysteria in me was pushing the words out, and they sounded more like Turkish than English. The Shrivers were understanding. Eunice let out a laugh that was free and contagious. It got everybody laughing, and we finished the meal in wild humor.

When it was bedtime, Maria Shriver, who was then eight, asked me to come to her room because she was having a slumber party with her cousins. She wanted me to get into bed with them and tell stories. I did. I climbed in and told them some outlandish and some dramatic tales. While I was between stories, Maria asked if I was Catholic.

I said, "No, and I don't even know if I believe in God."

Then Maria said, "Why don't you come to church with me in the morning? Maybe it will help you find out what you think and how you feel about it." *And I thought, What a smart little eight-year-old child this is.*

"I'd love to," I said.

We then said our good nights, and I went back to my little room with the four-poster bed and went to sleep. Something happened that night that had been occurring on and off for several months. During the night, I'm basically asleep, but my eyes are open. In the dark I see someone coming toward me. My scalp is tingling I'd be so frightened, and at the top of my lungs, I start screaming, "No, no, no! Get out! Get out! Help! Help!!"

It happened that night. I went through the full opera, screaming at the nonexistent creature, cringing, and carrying on till I wore myself out and eventually went back to sleep. The next morning, when I awoke, I realized that Eunice was right next door to me. I tried to imagine why she hadn't come in to see what was wrong. *Oh, my God,* I thought. Maybe she didn't come in, because she thought Sarge had come into my room. That's how wildly my mind was racing and how frenzied my imagination became. The whole idea was laughable. Sarge is a wonderful husband and father.

Suddenly I realized I was supposed to go to church with Maria. I jumped out of bed and tore down the hallway. I came to the top of the stairs and saw Eunice just going out the front door.

"Eunice!" I called. "Wait!"

She stopped.

I said, "What will I do? I told Maria I'd go to church with her."

"It's all right. Just stay home," she called up to me.

"Pray for me," I said.

"I will. Don't worry," she replied and waved good-bye as she went out the door.

I was miserable that I didn't do what I'd said I was going to do, but both Eunice and Maria were gracious to me. Both have been dear friends through the years. Both are extraordinary, outstanding women.

Some months later Eunice, Sarge, Eunice's sister Jean, Rose Kennedy, the matriarch of the Kennedy clan, and George and I were crowded into a limousine on a cold night in New York. We were in formal dress and were on our way to the world premiere of a film. I don't remember the name of the film, because it's crowded out by the memory of something that happened on the way to it. We'd had a wonderful dinner together, and the atmosphere inside the limousine was warm and chummy. During a lull in the conversation, I said, "Mrs. Kennedy, there's something I'm really curious about. Did you nurse your children?"

It was as if I'd said I thought Communism was a great form of government. No one knew where to look. Eunice stared out the window. After what seemed like a weeklong silence, Rose Kennedy spoke.

"I've never talked about this before," she said, "especially not with my children." There was another pause, in which I thought I was going to be arrested for asking that question. Then Mrs. Kennedy continued. "Of course, I nursed them. Anything else would have been unthinkable. I wanted my children to grow up healthy and natural. Of course, I nursed them."

All her kids had wanted to know if they'd been breastfed, but in all the years, they'd never had the gumption to ask. Eunice told me later how stunned she and Jean and Sarge had been when I popped that daisy cutter of a question. She then thanked me and said how good it was to know after all those years.

I got an invitation to visit the Kennedy's, on another occasion when I was in New York, doing a television show. My daughter, Dinah, was with me. On our last day of shooting, Sarge called and invited us up to the Cape. The next morning Dinah and I were headed for Cape Cod. As soon as we got there Ethel Kennedy invited us out for an afternoon sail.

She picked us up and took us to the pier where the small sailboat was waiting. Ethel is an outstanding woman, cheerful and smart and concerned. And a hell of a sailor. There was a healthy breeze blowing, and Ethel showed her skill. She weaved through the waves and the currents expertly. She'd get the boat on a port tack, then on a starboard tack, and then she'd change tacks again, always propelling us forward. It was a stirring ride.

As we pulled into the harbor, a larger sailboat came too close to us. It hit us, and the masts got tangled together. It looked like our mast was going to be torn off and fall on top of us. Ethel moved like a puma, leaping to the other side of the boat, where Dinah sat, and covering Dinah's body with hers. She stayed there, protecting Dinah, until it was clear the mast was going to remain intact. Hers was quiet heroism, but in truth, that's what you expect when you're among the Kennedys.

When Sarge was the vice presidential candidate on the Democratic ticket with George McGovern in 1972 and was campaigning in Los Angeles, he stayed with us. It was about seven years after the Watts Riots, and Sarge brought the leaders of the riots to the house. That was high drama: these were angry young men who had vowed to ignite Beverly Hills and Brentwood, where we lived. Now they were in our home. It turned out to be a memorable day. We talked, played football on the back lawn, and discussed the riots. Everyone there got to know everyone else in more than a surface way.

I made chili for lunch, and it was praised by all. There's a history behind that chili lunch. The sponsors of the theater George ran in East Rochester, New York, were the Volunteer Fire Department. One afternoon I invited the firemen and their wives to lunch. I made chili, and it got a bit scorched. I decided to solve the problem by quartering potatoes, putting them in the chili to soak up the scorched taste, and then removing them. It panned out, I got all kinds of compliments on my unusual-tasting chili.

Years later, when we were living in Brentwood, Elizabeth Taylor was among our dinner guests one night. And, yup, I made chili. At that time the most famous restaurant in Beverly Hills was Chasen's, and Chasen's was world famous for having the best chili anywhere. When we sat down to dinner, Elizabeth dug right in. After a couple of bites of the chili, she turned to me and said, "Cloris, I can't believe how good this is. It's got that special flavor that Chasen's chili has. I thought you must have had it delivered from there. How did you do it?"

I didn't tell her the truth, that I had put no meat in it. I had cooked the beans three different ways to create the sense that there was meat, but there wasn't. My success that day in bringing new methods to chili cooking had its roots in the lunch I'd prepared for the volunteer firemen in East Rochester, New York. So if you come to my house, and we're having chili, you'll know you're eating something that was given four stars by both Elizabeth Taylor and the volunteer firemen of East Rochester.

Back to Teddy. A few days after I won my Oscar, Teddy called and invited me to Washington. I flew in, and an enchanted time began, I felt like I was in one of those Leslie Caron movies, *Gigi* or *Lili*. Teddy took me to the in restaurants, to the National Gallery, and to the Senate, where he introduced some new legislation. We drove around the city in his convertible, with the top down. It was rare, energetic, and unique. I've never been with any of the Kennedys when the air didn't seem supercharged, when there wasn't something competitive to get involved in.

Tonight I was enveloped in sadness when, on television, I saw Teddy being supported as he hobbled into his house. Here was the last of the Kennedy men, that exceptional group of males who so valiantly served our country.

Notes On Another President

Speaking of men who served our country, in 1959 I was in New York to do a live television show, *General Electric Theater,* with Ronald Reagan. I met the cast, we rehearsed, and on the day of the show, we did a dress rehearsal. After it, Ron, or Dutch, as everybody used to call him, and I went to dinner together. As we stepped along the New York sidewalk, I thought back to when I was seventeen in Des Moines and had my own radio show, that "advice to women" half-hour. At our station we thought Dutch Reagan, then a sportscaster on the other station, WHO, was kind of square. That was my only memory of him.

So, fifteen years later, there we were, Dutch and me, walking to a New York restaurant. We came to a corner, and something—I can only use the word *magical*—happened. He took my arm and ushered me across the street. He did this in no ordinary way. He was gallant. All he did was take my arm, but it was so noble, so natural. I was really affected by the man, the soul, he was.

Dinner was enjoyable, and my vision of Dutch now

growing different from what it had been before. After
dinner we went back to do the show at NBC. Remember,
this was live television. No videotape. No film. Once the
show started, the actors had to put all their words and all
their moves together gracefully and fit them into exactly
one hour.

The show was set in the South in the summer. At a certain point, rain and fog were to roll in. The special-effects
man had figured out how to create this weather change:
he'd pour cold water on the side flaps of the lights beside
the camera. I guess he didn't rehearse the trick, because
when we were right there in front of the cameras and he
threw the cold water on the hot flaps, a horrible, belching
noise erupted in the studio. It got louder and louder, and
we couldn't hear each other. As seems to be my custom, I
uttered something unconnected to anything in the script.
I heard myself say, "Well, I'm just going to run my fingers
through the water."

The ad-lib didn't make sense, but Dutch wasn't disturbed
by it, and he wasn't knocked off balance by the special-effects
calamity. He knew his lines and he said them calmly and
his "take command" presence steered us out of the darkness. There was the most extraordinary manliness about
him. Impressed as I was by Dutch Reagan during that handful of days, I never could've imagined, it couldn't have entered my mind, that he would become president of the
United States.

There is another little story attached to Ronald Reagan
and the presidency. When I lived in Brentwood, California, I'd often go down to the Brentwood Country Mart

and have a juice or buy what we needed for the house. It was a social place as well as a market. One afternoon, when I was standing by the shelves of tomato cans—I remember that's where I was—someone came bustling around the corner. Nancy Reagan. I didn't know her, but from what I'd seen of her, I thought she was rather cold.

I didn't want my face to show what I was thinking, so I put on a squeaky, sunny countenance and said, "Hi, Nancy."

She said, "Oh, Cloris. Hi." I guess we had met before. That's what her tone suggested.

We chatted a minute, good to see you, yes, you too, that sort of thing and then out of my mouth came, "Well, what do you think?"

The question was connected to nothing, and she kind of pushed her shoulders up, as if to say, "I don't know." But there was a little secretive smile on her lips, too.

Since I didn't know what I'd meant when I asked the question, it was hard to know what she meant when she gave that silent response. So I said, "Really?" with my eyebrows raised, as if she'd laid some wondrous piece of information on me.

Then she made that secretive smile again, that seemed to say, "I know but I'm not going to say."

And I exclaimed, "Oh, my gosh!" Then we both nodded as if something highly confidential had passed between us, said our good-byes, and left the Brentwood Country Mart.

A couple of days later, I was on *The Tonight Show*, and Johnny Carson asked me what was new, what I was doing. I gave the little secretive smile I'd copied from Nancy, because by now I had a strong sense of what the silent shrugs and raised eyebrows were all about. I told Johnny that I'd met with Mrs. Reagan, and I had some powerhouse political news no one else possessed—Ronald Reagan was going to run for president.

Immediately, there was applause and cheers and jeers in the audience. Johnny leaned forward and asked me how in the world I had got hold of such inside political stuff and no one else had heard about it. I gave him that wise little smile Nancy and I had perfected and didn't say anything more. I just sat there like a Cheshire cat. My insides were churning, because I was betting the farm on what I'd discerned was the message Nancy was giving me in our cave woman grunts beside the tomato cans at the Brentwood Country Mart. Imagine the semidivine status I was accorded when, two weeks later, Ronald Reagan declared his candidacy for the office of president of the United States.

I'm still not sure if Nancy was telling me what I'd decided she was telling me or if I'd had a mystical séance with a gypsy soothsayer inside me.

Another Presidential Tidbit

I n 1992 I was in St. Louis, appearing in *Show Boat*. Bill Clinton had just been elected president. It seemed to me that his body had become distorted from eating on the campaign trail, grabbing and snacking, and I thought I could help him lose weight. I called Hillary, whom I'd never met but whose number I had somehow got, and talked to her secretary for probably forty-five minutes. It was a sustained, leisurely chat, and at the end I left the message for Hillary that I thought I could get our new president to lose a few pounds.

Two days later my phone rang, and a woman's voice said, "Cloris? Cloris, this is Hillary."

For a stunned moment, I forgot what I had called her about, but swiftly I remembered. "Hillary," I said, "how good of you to call. I just wanted to offer to come to the White House as soon as you move in and cook a few meals in the kitchen, some little things that I think the president would enjoy eating and would help him lose the weight he's put on. I'll keep a bag over my head the entire time so no one will recognize me. Then I'll sneak away quietly, and no one will ever know I was there."

After that we talked for nearly an hour. We had a funny, open, and honest exchange. She'd seen me on television, and of course, I'd seen her all over the place. Hillary couldn't have been nicer during our conversation, and she didn't at all resent me calling her husband fat.

A Little More About The Present

I mentioned at the beginning some of the things that are keeping me busy. Two of them stand out, winning my ninth Emmy and becoming a great-grandmother. I paused to consider what meaning those two events hold for me. The first shows that I'm not only still working, but I can still duke it out with the twenty-two-, forty-two-, and sixty-two-year-olds, who are after the same awards I am.

The second, becoming a great-grandmother, is a statistic that brings a special clarity to your life. It says you have already walked most of the road of your life. You are now where those odd-looking others were, the old ones you stared at when you were a child. An eighty-year-old person back then was someone who took half a minute to turn around when you called to her from behind. At the age of seven, I decided I would never be like that. No way. Uh-uh. Not me. And yet, almost without noticing, with silent thunder, I've pulled into the eighties depot. And a new question arises. What now?

Do I get a different wardrobe, put on fleece-lined slippers and wear a bathrobe most of the day? Should I walk differently, put one hand on the small of my back, grab the top of a chair with the other, and pull myself toward the kitchen?

Should I heed those mortuary commercials in which two elder models pretend unconvincingly to be husband and wife, and she flashes her dentures at him, pats him on his rheumatoid knee, and says, "You know, dear, we really should talk about these things."

And he replies, "Well, Helen, you've always been the one for 'advanced planning.'" He makes quote marks in the air. "And you haven't been wrong yet, so this bozo's going with you to get that comfort cot for eternity."

"Oh, Matt," she says. "You're so dear. You make me fall in love all over again. Careful. Don't trip on that open grave."

Should I have my business manager call the mortuary and negotiate for a plot, maybe a large plot, so the dead who follow me can lie eternally—or at least until the cemetery is sold—beside me?

If I took that road, there would be questions I'd have to answer. Would I want to lie near the freeway, in a less expensive plot? Would I want to be near one of those faux angels, who are welcoming you not only to your final resting place, but to contribute to the bottom line of the mortuary company who bought the statue on sale in Argentina?

And what about incineration, or cremation, as they like to euphemize it? I've never understood why *cremation* is a better word than *incineration*. To be cremated sounds like you wind up in a half-and-half milk carton. Should I take that route? Should I leave an urn with ashes alleged to be mine, which will sit on my daughter Dinah's make-up table?

Along with those somber considerations, there are some special joys in being a great-grandmother. The other day I was sitting in my living room, with my great-grandson lying in my lap. My granddaughter, Hallelujah, who is now three years old, climbed onto the stool in front of me. She watched the baby, and then she looked at me and said, "Grandma, he's getting so big."

"He's something, isn't he?" I replied.

I think I must've been waiting years for this moment, because I remembered a song I've always loved from the musical *Fanny*, called "Love Is a Very Light Thing." I sang it to Hallelujah.

To come back to the subject of cremations and burial places just for a moment, after I had conjured with the possibilities for a while, well, as long as I was able to, which was a little under seven minutes, I was ready to talk about something else. Here's a little sidebar.

The Chaplin Connection

During World War II, George was in military school with Charlie Chaplin's two sons with Lita Grey, Charlie Jr. and Sydney. They were like the Three Musketeers, always together, all for one and one for all, inseparable. Charlie Jr. has been dead these many years, but today Sydney and George are still pillars of each other's lives.

Charlie Chaplin loved to play tennis, and he had a spectacular court at his home in Beverly Hills. During the war, it pretty much lay idle, since his tennis buddies, movie stars, directors, and writers were serving in the military. George was an excellent young tennis player, so two or three times a week, Mr. Chaplin's English butler, Edward, would call George's mother and say, "Mr. Chaplin would like George for tennis this afternoon if that can be arranged."

"It could," George's mother would say, and a Rolls-Royce would arrive to carry George to the Chaplin manor. George had only recently arrived from New York. He was a kid from PS 166 on Columbus Avenue on the Upper West Side, so going to Charlie Chaplin's house to play tennis with the man whose films he had been watching with awe since he was a little child was an out-of-body experience.

George soon became accustomed to the tennis occasions. After they'd played, Mr. Chaplin and he would sit alone and talk about life, the war, acting, and seeing Europe, which Chaplin recommended George do as soon as the war was over, and they had long discussions about Communism. George would try to persuade Chaplin out of his Communist leanings.

After the war, Sydney and George were founding members of the Circle Theater in Hollywood. Charlie Chaplin stopped by frequently to nurture the enterprise and give advice. Later, when I was in New York, pursuing my career, Sydney was building a Broadway success of his own. He played the lead opposite Judy Holliday in the 1956 Broadway musical *Bells Are Ringing*, then won the Tony for Best Actor in a Musical for his performance. He was nominated for a Tony for his performance opposite Barbra Streisand in *Funny Girl* in 1964.

I discussed earlier my experiences at the Actors Studio. In October of 1951, Charlie Chaplin came to see members of the Studio at work. We were introduced to this giant icon, and he spent the entire afternoon watching us do our scenes. A couple of days later, he sent a letter to the administrator of the Studio. It reads in part: "Of all the girls you were kind enough to arrange for me to interview, the one who stands out most is Cloris Leachman."

I don't remember ever seeing that letter; it was only as

we were doing research for this book that somebody handed it to me. Do you know what it's like to clean out your files and come across an old letter or photograph? You stop right there, lost in that moment, where you are. That's how it was when I saw Charlie Chaplin's letter. It was another Chaplin contact, but one I'd known nothing about.

The intertwining of George's life and mine with Charlie Chaplin had a wow finish twenty years later, when I won my Oscar. Talk about a night to remember . . . I don't recall it step-by-step, hour by hour. It's more like images in ascending and descending balloons, images of people cheering and waving, of rows of Hollywood's elite listening and looking glamorous. I'd asked George to go with me. It didn't matter that we were separated; he was the one to be there. I had on a beautiful gown. I'd tried it on and made sure it "walked." In case I did have to walk up to the stage, I wanted a gown that, well, walked with me, one that was graceful from all angles. And I had a gorgeous white full-length coat, which, it turned out, I never put on. The chauffeur carried it the whole night.

I didn't think I'd win an Oscar that night. Ellen Burstyn had just won the New York Drama Critics Circle Award, and Ann-Margret had won the Golden Globe. Also, Ellen and I were in the same movie, and that meant that probably neither of us would get it. My mind flipped back to when Ellen and I became friends on the little plane going from Wichita to our location in Texas. She was trying to figure out what her name was going to be; it wasn't Ellen Burstyn at that point. The entire time during filming, we talked with Texas accents on camera and off. We shared wonderful hours. . . .

George and I were in our seats. It was getting close to my category, and I leaned over to him and said, "What if I win? What will I say?"

He said, "You'll think of something, babe."

"No, I won't," I said. "My mind's a blank. I've been thinking about my teachers, Helen Fouts Cahoon, Lillian Rosedale Goodman, Cornelia Williams Hurlburt. What funny names they all had. I don't even know how to spell them."

Then I heard, "And the winner is . . . Cloris Leachman!" I looked up and thought, did they just say the names of the nominees? Then there was an uproar, and the spotlight was on me. I part dashed, part trotted up to the stage. The dress was perfect; it walked with me. I was excited, thrilled, and happy. I ad-libbed my speech and was able to talk about everything: my teachers, my joy at winning, my feeling that we are all part of each other.

I have pictures of me holding my trophy and of Charlie Chaplin and me, both with our trophies, his the Lifetime Achievement Award. He was finally being recognized by the Academy of Motion Picture Arts and Sciences for his massive contributions not only to the film industry but to the lives of the millions who had dissolved in laughter and in tears at his performances.

So Charlie, the Little Tramp from England; Cloris, the nonconforming kid from the outskirts of Des Moines; and Sydney and George had a sentimental reunion and a very special evening together. The elation carried us through the gala party we attended after the ceremony. Practically everyone I'd ever seen in a movie or heard about was there that night. It was all Hollywood glamour and gorgeous gowns and handsome guys.

Receiving the Oscar was a signal honor, but it was as much an honor to spend time that evening with Charlie Chaplin. No one had as great an impact on the movie industry as he had; in fact he, more than any other person, gave shape to the industry in its earliest days. It was sublime to be his fellow professional that evening. During one of our conversations, he told me about the difficulties he faced when he started in the business. He'd begun working in pantomime companies and music halls, but he wanted to be an actor. He was aware from his childhood that he was short, that his head was too big for his body, and his teeth were too big for his head. But he forced himself to overcome his timidity and used his creative powers to try to audition for anything that was being produced.

He wangled a reading for a role in a new play. When he arrived at the production office, the producer and the director took one look at him and said, "Thank you for coming, but you wouldn't be at all right for the role we're casting."

Undeterred, Chaplin said to the producer, "Could I ask what the role is?"

"The man is a banker," the producer responded in a way that said it would be laughable for this diminutive, oddly made man in front of him to try to portray a banker.

"This is uncanny," Chaplin said, a look of eerie surprise on his face. "That's the only kind of role I ever play. Can we just have a look at the script?"

The nonplussed producer handed him the script. Chaplin celebrated its merits as he looked through it— then suggested that maybe just as an exercise, he should read for them. By this time the producer had forgotten how to say no, so Chaplin read and, owing mostly to his chutzpah, as he put it, got the part. The ploy didn't always work, Chaplin told me, but it was one of the techniques he developed to move up in the industry.

What came next—and was the culmination of our time together that evening—was, I'm afraid, pure me. "Mr. Chaplin," I said, "we've had such a memorable evening together, I'm going to do what I bet nobody else in this building would have the balls to do." I got up, walked ten paces away, and came toward him, doing an imitation of his famous Little Tramp, twirling cane and all. I was at my best, and Chaplin turned red, laughing. There was only one possible way to finish it off; I sat on his lap. To make a really hard appraisal, I'm not sure my imitation of the Little Tramp that night wasn't more Oscar worthy than my performance as Ruth Popper.

Love, Marriage, and All That Comes After

Through the years, one man has been—I'm not sure which words to use—partner, monorail, love of my life, maybe all those things. He and I met, courted, married, had three children, separated, came together again, and produced two more children. Six years later we divorced, he's specific that divorce in our case was a transference out of a legal vehicle, not the termination of our care and concern for each other. Those would not perish. I'm smiling. What could better illustrate the depth of our relationship than the fact that he helped me write this book?

He and I have laughed together as we have with no one else, shared the heart of the entertainment world in a way only our own, cried together as we read an Edna St. Vincent Millay poem, and stood in awe in front of Velázquez's painting *Las Meninas* at the Prado in Madrid. We've shared dinners with scientists and social workers, cardinals and atheists, defense ministers and drug dealers.

And we have, with the talent and ingenuity given to

both of us, brought to each other pain, suffering, and sadness of an intensity that no other force, no other person, could supply. But here we are today, still shaping and sharing pieces of life; still sorrowful over what we didn't, wouldn't, couldn't give each other; still uncertain about why those things weren't given; still marvelously enraptured when we're together. . . .

People say about us, "Obviously, they're connected to each other. What went wrong?" I don't think that's the right question. It presumes there's a single right way to be married, and in that right way, the two people are expected to live within a set of social and legal totems. Is that the natural way? Why isn't it right for two people to have an unbreakable tie throughout their lives and also be interested in, and excited, and fascinated by, others? I wonder how it materialized, this idea that two people should exchange marriage vows, then step into a closet whose tight dimensions were formed by the words they just spoke.

"Do you, Roger, take this woman, Marla, to love and to cherish, in sickness and in health? And will you keep your Groucho Marx leer off the butts of all other chicks, saving your orbs for only her fair curves till death do you part?" Then, when there's an apparent breach of this behavioral agreement, people say, "Oh, oh, it's gone wrong." But what if there's been no lessening of the two people's regard for each other, no dilution of their will to love and protect each other?

I don't know the answer to this question. If I did, I would have let the world know long ago. What I know for certain is that George Englund and I are two individuals who have shared life's journey, have been curious and have held hands through all of it, and have, along the way, weaved an unseverable tie.

One of us will die before the other. Oh, what calamity then. If George leaves this world first—it's hard even to write those words—birds will stop singing and lower their heads, gravity will let go, what holds my life together will be mist. I don't know what sounds I will make, how my face will alter, what my arms will do. I can't imagine going to his funeral, then going home, going anywhere. There will be nowhere in the world to go where there aren't endless tears, where I will walk without stumbling.

If I die first, what will George feel, experience? I'd almost rather he died before I do, so he won't go through that awful mystery. I hate death; I hate that we have to die. Who ever thought up that rotten idea? No, there is no imagining what will befall the other when one of us dies.

So when I write about my personal life and the parallel path of my career, it will be apparent that all of it has been touched by, affected by, sometimes consumed by my relationship with George Englund. Wherever we've been—no matter with whom we've dined or danced or lain beside— the tie that holds us has never weakened. And during the remainder of this life, it never will.

Since the beginning, there has been a madcap aspect to us. One incident pushes up out of the earth of my mind now. George had taught himself how to blow bubbles from his saliva in military school. He'd form them under his tongue, and during inspections, when the battalion was standing at attention, he'd release them and they'd sail aloft. The inspecting officer would have no idea where they'd come from. They'd just appear randomly, with no apparent origin; and not infrequently, they would burst on the inspecting officer's tunic.

One summer evening George and I were standing on the west side of Fifth Avenue, by Central Park, waiting to take the bus to a restaurant downtown. While we were standing there, George blew a bubble. A zephyrlike breeze carried it my way, and it burst on my neck.

"Don't do that, honey," I said.

"Do what?" he responded, with raised eyebrows, knowing full well what I was talking about. Then he blew another bubble.

"I don't like those bubbles hitting my neck and getting me wet," I protested.

"What bubbles?" And he blew another one, and the same breeze carried it to the same place on my neck, and it burst and got me wet the same way.

"Just don't blow any more, okay? It's sick. It's saliva. I hate them."

"This is America, babe. The pursuit of happiness is our birthright. That's all I'm doing. Pursuing a little happiness."

This time, showing his full dexterity, he blew two bubbles, and, yes, both landed on me. I stepped up next to him and spit on his neck. In a flash he spat back at me, and immediately I whipped him another one. Now the battle was on. We were laughing so hard, we could hardly get our lips in the right shape to spit. I spat a last bit of saliva, then ran to a drinking fountain nearby. I took a huge gulp of water, and as he came up behind me, I spun around and got him full in the face. Now it was a free-for-all. We were filling up and dousing each other when the bus pulled up.

Laughing and hugging each other, we got aboard, still captive to the hilarity and insanity of what we'd been doing. Our upper clothes were pretty well soaked, but we were lost in the crazy fun. The bus was full, so we had to hang on to straps. George hugged me, then gave me a kiss. When we finished kissing, I felt eyes on me. I looked over and saw this Catholic priest watching us. He was smiling merrily and nodding his head from side to side in enjoyment of what he was seeing. Then the most magical thing happened. With that wonderful smile on his face and a look of endearing approval, the priest made the sign of the cross over us. Neither of us is a churchgoer, but that moment glistened with sacredness. It glistens now in my memory. Doing the most childish, frivolous things, George and I could sound the flutes and piccolos, the timpani of being human.

Georgie is our third son. We call him Georgie or Junior to distinguish between him and his father. There was no particular reason we called him George, except that he was the third boy, and we realized that neither of his brothers had been named after their father, so this might be a good time to do it. Georgie inherited our madhouse DNA. He has the same love of travesty, the same talent for high riposte and low humor. The three of us together are a trio of gibbons. Georgie will make a pun; then George will top it. Then I'll join in, and we're off into a barnyard scramble, laughing, howling, cackling. It's something that happens to that degree only among the three of us.

Here's what I said about George in an *Esquire* interview in 2008. "A publicist at MGM once said to me about another actress, 'She can't come near your asshole.' That's what I say about George. No man I ever knew could come near his asshole. He's a world-class guy, an exceptional, rare person. And he loves me, too. I'm number one with him. He has a girlfriend now, Kathryn Amoroso. She takes wonderful care of him, and he loves her. But I'm still the one. I have always loved him and always admired him, and I always will."

Before George, there was Hy Sobiloff.

In 1947 I was living at the Barbizon Hotel For Women. I was in the drugstore one day, and the man behind the counter introduced me to the man to whom he was talking. We got into a conversation, and he seemed interesting. He read poetry. Things like that. We went out to lunch, then later to dinner, and he introduced me to one of his friends, a man named Hy Sobiloff. Hy was remarkable. I saw that right away.

Hy and I dined several times, and soon I was seeing him almost every night. Hy was a wonderful dancer; he loved to dance, and so did I. When I was finished at the theater, a limousine would pick me up and take me to Hy, then we'd go to El Morocco or the Blue Angel or some other soigné cabaret and have dinner and dance. It was a top-drawer life.

Hy was a self-made businessman and wealthy. He was

also a poet. He had a gorgeous apartment on upper Fifth Avenue, opposite the Metropolitan Museum of Art. Though we were together almost every night, we didn't live together. I kept my own apartment. Every summer Hy would charter a yacht, and we'd invite our friends aboard. Often we'd sail out to Montauk, at the eastern tip of Long Island. We were like those wealthy folks in a 1930s movie, with our champagne, chatter, merriment.

I remember Hy with the greatest fondness. I'll never forget his wonderful voice and laugh, and how compellingly he told stories. He was a loving, generous, good man.

In 1949 I was in *Come Back, Little Sheba* with Shirley Booth. We played in Westport prior to coming to Broadway, and Tallulah Bankhead came to see the play. She was maybe the most flamboyant actress of her day. Tallulah came backstage, with tears in her eyes, took my hand, and said, "You are the Jeanne Eagels of today!" I knew it was a compliment, but at the time I didn't know who Jeanne Eagels was. I later found out she was a legendary actress of the 1920s. Talullah went on. "You are marvelous beyond words, but, darling, you have to change your name."

Hy's yacht was berthed at a marina on the East River, so we invited Miss Bankhead aboard and went for a sail. She was famous for her drinking, and that night we were treated to a vivid illustration of how much she could put away. Tallulah Bankhead would create her own alcoholic ballroom and dance through it, unrestrained. Her major theme of the evening was that I had to change my name.

"Cloris Leachman," she crowed, "too long. Too many syllables. Too unknown. Clorox Bleachman would be better. You can't even fit it on the marquee in front of a theater."

I sort of caught her drift. Claiborne is my youngest sister's name. She was named after William Claiborne, who was a governor, so I figured maybe I could be something Claiborne. I was born in April, so I could be April Claiborne. Tallulah called me April that evening, shrieking it so loudly, it could be heard on the shoreline. But April didn't work; I was definitely not an April.

When I went to the Actors Studio the next day, I talked about Madame Bankhead's rant. They all agreed with her. "You have to change your name! You have to!," they cried. It was a unanimous opinion. So right there we got out the New York phone book. I opened it up to the *Ls*, closed my eyes, and put my finger on the page. I opened my eyes, and the name under my finger was Leavitt. It was miraculous. That translated to "Leave it!" *This is no accident*, I thought. *The god of monikers is talking, and he says leave it. Okay, I'll leave it.*

When I got to Hollywood, the subject came up again. People said I should not only change my name, I should have my nose shortened. I emphatically didn't want to do either, and that's why I'm still Cloris Leachman with a big nose.

Hy had been married since he was very young; he was twenty when his girlfriend became pregnant. They had a son, who was thirteen years old when I met Hy. The wife seemed to be a psychological mess. She was schizophrenic and was in and out of hospitals, and on one occasion she tried to kill her son. The boy was afraid for his life; he was even afraid to get in the elevator with his mother. He was afraid to do anything.

The situation upset Hy terribly, and he cried about it for long hours during the night. Though his former wife had custody of his son, he decided he had to take over. He found out everything he needed to know about the boy's condition and how to help him. Hy greatly improved the quality of his son's life. I heard that years later, when the boy had grown up, he married the doctor who had treated him, and last I heard they were living happily in Missouri.

Though Hy and I were very close, there were difficulties. He was thirteen years older than I, his friends were thirteen years older than I. I was the little girl in the crowd, always sitting on Hy's lap.

The fact that Hy was Jewish had no relevance to me. However, anti-Semitism was still an issue in the country at that time, maybe especially in the Midwest, but my parents never mentioned anything about Hy being Jewish or being older than me. They were wonderful with Hy. The only negative I ever heard in that regard was from Grandma Leachman, who once said, "Is Cloris still with that Jew in New York?" I remember driving through Miami with Hy and seeing NO JEWS ALLOWED in one hotel after another.

The major difficulty between Hy and me was his jealousy. He was certain I'd leave him, that I'd run off to Hollywood or run away and get married. He invented every kind of disloyalty scenario.

Hy always sent me a white orchid when I opened in a new play. On the opening night of the 1952 Broadway play

Dear Barbarians, he not only sent the white orchid, he had my parents brought to the theater in a limousine. The opening was a success, and we went to a gala party afterward.

When Mama and Daddy and I were back in my apartment, Hy and I got into a terrible argument over the phone—it was one of his immersions in jealousy—and I was crying. That upset Daddy terribly, and he waved to me to get off the phone. When I did, he said, "End it. Just end it!" I called Hy the next day, and he agreed we should break up. So we did. Just like that.

So often in life, relationships don't end with a final good-bye; ours didn't. Fifteen years later, I was in New York, staying in the Plaza Hotel. I took the elevator down and was walking through the lobby, and there, coming across the lobby in the opposite direction, was Hy. We hadn't seen or spoken to each other in all those years, and we both almost broke down with emotion when we saw each other. We went into the Oak Room, the Plaza's beautiful restaurant, and talked and cried. I said, "Oh, Hy, I didn't take very good care of you in those years." His response was to tell me what an inspiration I had been for him always.

He had a home in the Bahamas, and he asked me to come and visit him there. I thought it was important to do it, and I wanted to do it. I invited Claiborne, my sister, and her son Berkely to accompany me and my three boys down to Hy's house in the Bahamas. It was a beautiful house, and everything around it sparkled: the sea, the tropical flowers, the enjoyment in everybody's eyes. During our stay, I sculpted a head of Hy, which everyone, especially Hy, thought was very lifelike. I had it nearly finished when I got called back to LA for a television show. Claiborne said she'd take Hy's head back, and she did.

Just about a year later, I was up in Oregon, with the family, visiting with Paul Newman and his family. I got a call one evening during our visit—it's funny I can't remember from whom—informing me that Hy had died. I immediately thought that it must have been from his years of drinking. I called Claiborne to tell her the news. She was deeply saddened. She knew my whole history with Hy. She was also shocked because the day before, she told me, the same day Hy had died, the little boy from upstairs had come down and pushed the eyes out of the clay head of Hy. I couldn't stop thinking about that strange, eerie coincidence.

The night after I broke up with Hy, I called Patsy Englund to see if we could have dinner together. At that time Patsy and I shared a dressing room for *As You Like It*. I first came to admire Patsy, and then I came to love her. She earned my admiration when, one afternoon during rehearsals, she and I went out for lunch and came back to the theater a few minutes late. Karl Nielsen, our very military stage manager, immediately reprimanded us and gave us a terse lecture on our responsibility to be on time. Patsy, unintimidated, spoke up. "Karl, you are absolutely right," she said. "It won't ever happen again."

That was the end of it. Given her straightforwardness, there was nothing else to say. Patsy seemed so admirable to me in so many ways, I wondered if she had a brother. She did. After the show one night, George, his and Patsy's stepfather, Ken Englund, and their friend Herb Sargent were walking toward Patsy and me. *What a handsome trio,* I thought. George and I were introduced, and we chatted for a few minutes. From that first moment, there was a connection between George and me.

George came intermittently to *As You Like It* and would appear backstage afterward and visit Patsy and me in our dressing room. I remember how he'd look at me in the mirror when I was taking off my make-up and washing my feet in the sink. One blizzardy night he offered to take me home. A friend of his had a car and would give us a lift.

When we got to my building, George and I stepped out of the car and said good night to the others. We didn't go in; we stood outside, talking. Snowflakes, bright against the black sky, fell soundlessly around us. We both said how we were drawn to each other and how maybe we should "single up." We agreed we would.

But the road ahead would have its twists and turns. First, we began seeing only each other, and after a few months we moved in together. Then a pattern emerged: something would happen, some misunderstanding, something that made it too difficult to live together, and we'd separate. It wasn't huge issues, like religion and atheism, or one of us being a Republican and the other a Democrat. It was less tangible than that. Certain things that I did drove George crazy. For instance, if you were in a Broadway show, you got paid every Friday night, not by check, but by cash, in a little envelope. That's how it was then; I don't know if it's the same today. I wasn't sure what to do with that money, so I'd just put it somewhere. George found out where. One evening he went to get some ice to put in his soft drink, and he opened the refrigerator door, then the little door to the compartment that held the ice trays. However, he couldn't get to the ice trays, because the compartment was full of hundred-dollar bills, about six weeks of my pay.

He came into the bedroom, where I was. "Babe," he said, "you've got to explain something to me. What inside you tells you to put your money in the ice trays in the refrigerator?"

I didn't have an answer. I didn't really know why it was so important. "What's wrong with keeping money in the ice trays?"

"Whoa," George said. "Do you really not know? There's a kind of nutty idea going around these days called putting your money in the bank. The reason is people know their money is safe there. It gains interest, and they can keep track of how much they have and what they've been spending it on."

That kind of discussion was of no interest to me. It was boring, boring, boring. I wanted George to stop talking and put his arms around me and hug me. I told him that. He tried. He held me, but it was tense. I really couldn't see then, and I still can't see now, why he'd want to talk about things like that when we could be having hugs.

George tried to do a self-analysis to determine why such matters were important to him. He said that first, the issue was one of practicality, efficiency, and secondly, it was about stature. I had a standing in the business, and he had none. I was already a star, and I could do what I wanted. I could be careless about my money. He, on the other hand, was without an identity. There was a humiliation factor involved, he said.

During one separation that lasted a year, I'd tell a girlfriend or a sorority sister who had come in from Chicago about this darling guy, George Englund, and I'd urge her to call him up, and hand out his number. After that year went by, while George and I were still in separation mode, I opened in a new play, *King of Hearts*. On opening night, after the performance, Mama and Daddy and I went to Pat's Chop House, a favorite actors' hangout. As we entered, I saw George's coat hanging on the rack and had a visceral response: I just knew he belonged to me, and I belonged to him.

Another thing that made George irresistible was how he treated his grandmother. Frequently, we'd all go to Pat's Chop House, and she'd accompany us. He loved her so, this little Jewish woman, when he hugged her, he'd pick her up off the ground and hold her. He talked to her like she was one of us, starting out in show business. She just loved it. She loved him as much as he loved her. The way he took care of her, I'll never forget that.

We started seeing each other again, and one night he took me to a little restaurant we both liked on Madison Avenue. After dinner we hailed a cab and went to the theater. When I'd finished the play, we went to see a movie, *The Red Shoes*. During the movie, he kissed me on the cheek, and tingling, a vibration, went through my whole body. We went back to my apartment, and my sister Mary was in my bed. George and I talked till six in the morning, both of us shaking from the cold and tiredness. The upshot was we decided to get married.

But at that point, drawn to each other as we were, we still didn't really know each other. Three months later, in the twisted way that life happens, we were in a Broadway play together, *Lo and Behold!* by John Patrick, who'd won the Pulitzer Prize for his play *The Teahouse of the August Moon*.

Lo and Behold! was directed by Burgess Meredith. The thing I remember most about that play was my, well, warfare with a character actress named Doro Merande. I had replaced another actress, who was a close friend of Doro's, so she didn't like me from the start. She and I played ghosts; she was an Indian, and I was a Southern belle. She would do things onstage to get even with me, she would move while I was talking or actively rock in a chair while I was doing my monologue. I have to hand it to her; she invented new, bizarre ways to shift attention away from me and onto herself.

The situation did not improve. It got worse, far worse, everybody in the cast was appalled at her behavior. One night she locked her leg so I couldn't get past her while I was supposed to be leaving the stage. I'm usually timid, I avoid confrontations, but she just plain pissed me off. The next night she worked the rocking chair harder than ever, and after we finished the scene and left the stage, I punched her in the arm. I ran up to George's dressing room for protection, because I was sure I was going to get a tomahawk in the head. I'd never done anything like that before.

Now, everyone in the cast was offended by Doro, so

Burgess called a meeting of the whole cast, including Doro. He was infuriated at what she'd been doing. He attacked her with deep anger, telling her that she had violated the dignity of the theater and of the cast of which she was a part, that she had dirtied the basic concept of human civility. He said one thing I'll never forget. "Somebody put a dish of pus on the floor in case she gets thirsty." Doro was reported to Actors' Equity, and the threat of being thrown out of a play by her own union for unacceptable behavior made her change her ways.

One of the other actors in *Lo and Behold!*, Paul Crabtree, had written and directed *A Story for a Sunday Evening*, the Broadway play in which I had my first starring role. Paul and George shared a dressing room, and when they were not onstage, they'd have extended conversations. Paul ran two summer theaters, one in East Rochester, New York, and the other in Fayetteville, just outside of Syracuse. When Paul heard that George wanted to get out of acting and become a producer and director, he invited George to be the managing director of the East Rochester Theater in the upcoming summer. We spent the summer in East Rochester. I'll talk about that shortly.

Burgess became a big part of our lives, and George and I both learned from him. He was not only a riveting actor and superb director, he was knowledgeable about all the arts. He had mature taste in everything, from paintings to Calder mobiles to fine wines, exotic cordials, and haute cuisine. Burgess had his own way of making salads. He'd take a head of purple cabbage, pull it apart manually, then pair it with a zesty dressing of his own creation. We'd eat the cabbage with our hands, accompanied by an herb-laden Mediterranean bread and glasses of one of his superb wines. I still make cabbage salad the way Burgess did.

One night, years later, George mentioned to Burgess that he was taking Jackie Onassis to dinner at "21." Burgess promptly offered to supply the wine. He did, from his own cellar at "21," a Richebourg, the finest of the Burgundies. He couldn't have chosen better. It made the meal, Jackie said, and she asked George to tell Burgess that after the first sip, she clicked glasses with George, then put hers down and applauded. She said their dinner was the best one she'd had since she'd returned from Greece.

Enough about Jackie. Back to me. It's been true throughout my entire adult life that sometimes I wear myself down to a nub. I don't know the specific cause. It could be because I'll stay up late, watching television or reading a book until six in the morning, then jump into the day and get virtually no sleep the following night. It's what I mentioned before. I push hard on the brake and the gas pedal at the same time. I'll be smiling about the delights life holds, then suddenly say, "Oh, God," and I'll be, as Shakespeare wrote, "like Niobe, all tears." And after the tears, laughter bubbles again.

During one of these periods, while George and I were together in New York, I had worked myself into a serious condition. George was deeply worried. The idea sprang into his mind to call his mother in California as I sat beside him.

"Muth," he said—that's what he called her, Muth—"you

know this girl I'm seeing, Cloris Leachman . . . she's in a bad state. She is worn out, weeping, has lost a lot of weight. I think the best remedy for her is to be out there with you. Is that okay?"

"Of course," Mabel said. "I'd love to have her. Put her on a plane." Just her response made me start to feel better.

The next day I left for California. Mabel Albertson met me at the airport and drove me to the handsome home in Benedict Canyon she and Ken Englund had built and where Patsy and George had grown up. From the moment I entered the house, I felt I had come home, and that something of great importance was starting. Something of importance *was* starting: Mabel would become the closest person to me in this life.

She was a successful actress. She'd done scads of television shows, playing Darrin's mother on *Bewitched*, and Margaret and Barbara's mother on the 1950s TV series *Those Whiting Girls* and appearing as a regular on several other series. Oddly, Mabel and I never had a chance to work together. It seems strange to me now. We should have at least once, but the opportunity never arose.

To me, Mabel's real creative life was in music. She played the piano with such easy intimacy, and when she sang and accompanied herself, she tugged at your emotions. She was inside the song. Oh, how she'd move you when she sang "Bill" from *Show Boat*. We spent hours at the piano, playing and singing our hearts out. We did songs from Gilbert and Sullivan, Noël Coward, Rodgers and Hart, Cole Porter. Mabel knew Yiddish songs, Russian songs, Irish songs, French songs—and we sang them all. Those were the three most healthful weeks of my life, and I came back to New York happy and stable.

Later on, when I was thirty-five and living in Los Angeles, Mabel was my redeemer again. I had asthma, arthritis, and terrible hay fever, I couldn't sleep more than forty-five minutes a night. I went to every kind of doctor but found no relief. I didn't know what was wrong. You'd shake my hand, and I'd scream, because my knuckles were so painful. I took two antihistamine pills four times a day and constantly used inhalers because I just couldn't breathe.

I was going to go to Mabel's for breakfast one morning, and I thought, *I can't put another thing in me until whatever's in me comes out.* I shouldn't have done it, but on the way I stopped at a toy store to buy something for my youngest son, Georgie. When I was in the store, I suddenly sensed I had terrible breath, something I'd never experienced before. I didn't understand what was wrong. I left the store and went right to Mabel's.

When I arrived, she made a glass of fresh-squeezed orange juice for me. Then she called a woman friend, a naturopath named Dorothy Rheingold. Dorothy told Mabel to keep me on nothing but orange juice and water all day. We followed her instructions exactly, and the next day she switched me to grapefruit juice, and then to watermelon juice. Each day I had a different juice.

By the end of the third day, I was voraciously hungry, and Mabel made some carrot juice, warmed it up, and put little pieces of avocado in it. The fourth day I wasn't hungry at all; my appetite was gone. I learned that by the fourth day, the appestat in your brain turns off, and you don't get hungry until what they call true hunger sets in about two weeks later. I ended up staying on that diet for ten days.

And I lost ten pounds. I couldn't afford to lose them, because I only weighed a hundred pounds when I started. But my skin was pure and clean, my eyes were electrified, and my hair was lustrous. It was just amazing. I felt wonderful; I felt alive. The meaning of the words "at one with the universe" flowed through me, and I felt I truly was part of the cosmic flow.

I remember this thought coming to me. *I guess I won't be eating meat anymore.* It wasn't a philosophical decision, and I didn't read nutrition books. I haven't had a bite of meat from that day to this.

After my first memorable stay with Mabel, I went back to New York and prepared for my next Broadway production, *The Crucible*, a play by Arthur Miller about the witch hunts in Salem, Massachusetts, in the late seventeenth century. I didn't really want to be in it, because it was so depressing. It had so much pain and darkness in it. But everybody, especially Liebling, said it was an important production, and it was important that I be in it.

Everything about the production seemed weird. The leading actress, Beatrice Straight, read the palms of all the women in the cast. Looking at mine, she said, "You're going to get a lot of money, you're going to go on a trip, and you're going to get married and have three children." George and I were separated at that point, so I couldn't imagine how that would happen . . . but it did.

Jed Harris, one of the most famous directors and producers on Broadway, was our director. I thought he was cuckoo. I was dating his son, and Harris ordered him not to see me. Neither of us knew why, and we continued seeing each other, anyway. I don't know how Jed Harris got such a sterling reputation, since in my opinion, he was certifiably nuts. He was nearly deaf, so he would come up next to you while you were saying your lines and act out what you were saying. Also, while he was working with one actor, the rest of us would head offstage, as was customary. No, sir. He wanted us to stay right there and watch him act as the actress next to him was saying her lines.

Finally, due to mutual antagonism, I got out of the play. Jed Harris's reason for firing me was he wanted someone who looked more the part; he felt I looked too sweet in a nun's costume. The girl who wanted desperately to take over my role, my understudy, would walk by the producers, with tight sweaters and pointed breasts, doing everything she could to get it. Before I left, I said to her, "You should have told me you wanted it. I would've just given it to you."

I called George and told him that I'd been fired and I was free. After *Lo and Behold!* closed, Paul Crabtree took the position for the winter season of managing director at the new Royal Poinciana Playhouse in Palm Beach, Florida. He asked George to be the assistant managing director. George was happy to accept. He'd be the front man for the theater and would direct half the shows. George knew how unhappy I'd been in *The Crucible*, so his response to my call was, "Come with me to Florida. You can be part of the resident company."

No more golden words could have been spoken. As we drove south, through the Carolinas, I was in a dither. I felt compelled to identify every animal we passed. I'd say, "Look. There's a baby calf. Look. A goat. Isn't he darling?" I ate and slept all the way down. I ate everything on my plate and George's plate, everything I could find, and then I'd go to sleep. A few weeks later, in Palm Beach, I went to the doctor and found out I was pregnant. The conception had taken place during our overnight stay in North Carolina.

I remembered I'd said to myself a couple of months before. *I'm twenty-five. It's time to get married and have a baby.* So I was at peace with the world. The plan was working. I had the baby part taken care of.

Everything was not in balance the same way for George. He wasn't ready to be married. He couldn't imagine turning away from the life he'd envisioned. He wanted to see the world, to know other cultures, to live among other peoples. One of the founders of the Royal Poinciana Playhouse was a man named Frank Hale. He recognized George's abilities, and he became not only a close friend but a father figure to George. I know that many a night after George had closed the theater, he and Frank would drive around and have something to eat, and the principal subject of conversation would be what to do about my pregnancy.

Meanwhile, the business of the theater had to get done every day. Palm Beach was then the wealthiest place per square foot on planet Earth. Its social conformation was impenetrable, and wealth alone would not gain you entrance to the fortress that was Palm Beach. It was a different time then: women promenaded in summer gowns along Worth Avenue and rode along the waterfront in pedicabs. There were unspoken rules, such as if your skin was black, you had to be over the bridge and off the island by 5:00 p.m.

Since George and the actors had been brought to Palm Beach by three of its most prominent residents, they were given access to the heart of the place and its culture, a privilege almost no one else had. We were welcomed at the Everglades Club, a bastion of social privilege—you couldn't get in there with a flamethrower if you weren't a member— and to many of the stellar homes. One day, at lunch at the Everglades, George ran into Peter Lawford, an old friend from his beach days in Santa Monica. Almost in unison, they asked each other the same question. "What are you doing here?"

"I'm assistant director at the Playhouse," George said. "How about you?"

"I'm going to get married here," Lawford said. "I'm marrying Patricia Kennedy."

Lawford did marry Pat Kennedy, and he became an intimate part of Jack Kennedy's presidency. As I mentioned earlier, we'd see him and Pat around town, and especially at Matteo's, a favorite Italian restaurant. Ironically, some years later, our son Adam became Lawford's attorney. After President Kennedy was killed, Lawford's star faded. He'd been closer to Jack than to other members of the Kennedy family, and when the glow of Camelot dimmed, Lawford's place in it was gone.

One night Adam called George and said that Lawford was in the hospital and was not doing well, and that he thought Lawford would benefit from a call from George. When George called the hospital, Lawford could not talk immediately, but when he did finally get to the phone, the first thing he said was, "George, we've got winners." That was an expression from the two-man volleyball games on the Santa Monica beach and was used when a team was next up to play. Their conversation wasn't long. Lawford was weak and, as noted, a long way from the glamour days of the Kennedy presidency. In 2007 we met Pat and Peter's son, Christopher Lawford, at the Palm Springs Book Festival. George did an "In Conversation," (a discussion) with Christopher about his new book, in which he tells of the advantages and difficulties of being a member of the Kennedy clan, and of the drug life he fell into and his climb to sobriety. Christopher now has a flourishing acting career.

Messmore Kendall was one of the three who had financed the building of the Royal Poinciana Playhouse. He owned the Capitol Theatre in New York, the Greyhound bus line, and a number of other large corporations. Mr. Kendall gave a party at his home for those of us who were running the Playhouse and performing there. It was an important night for George, and he was concerned—not without reason, I have to say—about what I might do.

"Babe," he said as we were driving to the Kendall mansion, "tonight let's not do anything weird. Know what I mean?"

"I'm not sure," I answered. "Tell me." Of course, I knew.

"These are very conservative people. Palm Beach is probably the most conservative place in the country, so, you know, nothing outlandish."

I was reassuring. "Don't worry. I'll sit quietly and nod at what everybody else is saying."

George rang the bell at the Kendall mansion, and the front door was opened by a butler in formal attire. Behind him stood Mr. Kendall, a man in his late eighties, handsome in a dinner jacket and looking every bit the patrician he was. He had a full head of gray hair and flowing eyebrows.

"Good evening, George," Mr. Kendall said, offering his hand.

"Good evening to you, Mr. Kendall. Thank you for inviting us," George said as he shook Mr. Kendall's hand. "And may I present Miss Cloris Leachman."

"Cloris, very happy to know you," Mr. Kendall said and nodded.

As I murmured my return greeting, I was looking at Mr. Kendall with a smile I couldn't suppress. Then it came out of me. "Oh, there's nothing in this world I love as much as bushy eyebrows, and those are the bestest, the bushiest. I've just got to run my hands through them." I stepped over to Mr. Kendall and sent my fingers through his eyebrows.

Mr. Kendall not only did not object, he actually appeared to be enjoying what I was doing. He stood there like a domesticated animal.

"Cloris, aren't you something?" Mr. Kendall finally said and smiled. "Come on. Let me find you a glass of champagne." He took my hand, and the two of us went gaily off. George followed us, smiling at incorrigible Cloris.

The issue of my pregnancy became more and more critical as the days passed. Abortion was illegal in those days—this was long before *Roe v. Wade*—and abortions were costly and difficult to arrange. For me, an abortion was not a consideration. I loved George, and I wanted to have his child. I flew up to New York to see a doctor and a psychiatrist. When they asked me what my feelings were about having an abortion, I told them exactly the truth. The message I brought back from them was that insisting that I have an abortion would have serious and possibly dangerous consequences.

George told me later that on the final night of discussing the matter with Frank Hale, Frank said, "I think you have to do it, kid. You have to give the child a name." That was another serious matter then; no woman of any stature would have a child out of wedlock. So Cloris Leachman and George Englund were going to be married at a date to be set.

After Palm Beach, George and I spent the summer in East Rochester, New York, where, as I mentioned earlier, he was the managing director of the Summer Playhouse. While we were there, we bought a Doberman pinscher and a 1937 Ford Phaeton, a four-door convertible sedan. We brought both the dog and the convertible sedan back to New York City. Our plan was that when my water broke, we would get in the car, and George would drive me to Doctors Hospital.

The system at the Playhouse was that a new star would come in every week, bringing with him or her the other principal actor. One week, Margaret O'Brien, a former child star, was to appear in a charming but antique play called *Peg o' My Heart*. Six days before she was to arrive, George got a call from her manager, saying her leading man was sick and unable to perform. That was hairy. It was the middle of summer. Where could you find an actor who could play a young English squire?

George spoke to every agent he could find, but their suggestions were neither many nor good. Going by his gut instinct, George hired an actor who had no substantial credits. It wasn't clear how much acting he'd actually done. One of the interns picked him up at the train station and brought him to the theater. He was a country boy and carried a squirrel rifle.

"Hi. I'm George. Well, we're glad you're here safe and sound," George greeted him.

"Glad I'm here, too."

"Tell me your last name again, Steve."

"McQueen."

And so it was. Steve McQueen would appear on our stage in East Rochester in his first acting role. At the beginning, he was shy and awkward, but even on that first day, I saw he had a magnetic quality, an insouciance, which,

not too many years later, would make him a star in television and films.

At this point, however, Steve McQueen was a bungling
beginner. His words didn't come out clearly. He didn't
know stage nomenclature, including such terms as up-
stage, downstage, stage right, and stage left. He was, for the
most part, bewildered by what was going on.

We'd had his squire's costume sent up from New York.
It consisted of a tweed jacket, knickers, knee-length hose,
shoes with large buckles, a high-collared shirt, a flowing
ascot, and, atop his head, a tweed cap. I took on the job of
getting him used to his costume. I put on the whole outfit
and paraded around the stage to show him how he could
be comfortable in it. I enjoyed the process because I could
see that Steve was getting the idea and coming to life.

When Margaret O'Brien arrived, she didn't know her
leading man was about to lose his acting virginity with her,
and due to Steve's improvements, she never found out.
On opening night, Steve didn't wholly resemble a country
squire, but that alluring quality was there, and the audience felt it. They liked him, and we had a big, fat success
on our hands.

Seven or eight years later, when we were all living in
Los Angeles, we would see the McQueens. Steve was by
then married to his beautiful wife, Neile. At one dinner
we decided to hire a yacht for the weekend and sail around
Catalina. When we got aboard, we found there was only
one good stateroom, the master cabin. The other was a
good deal smaller and less inviting. I suggested we flip a
coin to see who got the master cabin. All agreed, so I

flipped, and Steve called heads. It was tails. I immediately said we'd take the master cabin the first night, and Steve and Neile could have it the second night.

That first night on board the yacht, George and I were lulled into a beautiful sleep, and we didn't get up till almost noon. When we did, Steve was biting his nails. He was afraid we were going to sleep the whole day away, and he and Neile would never get into the cabin. We got that smoothed out.

We were about twelve miles offshore and George suggested that he and Steve get in the dinghy and have a look around. Steve had never been on the ocean before and was a little unnerved as he looked out at the choppy surface. He'd brought his rifle on board, and George told him to bring it along so if a great white shark attacked them, he could shoot it.

Neile and I watched from the deck. As soon as the dinghy separated from the yacht, Steve gripped the gunwales with both hands. George pointed the little craft head-on into the waves, and it glided up one side of the waves, shot off the top, then slid down into the ocean, ready for the next wave. Steve was out of his element, and he did everything but start to chatter. But he had a natural talent for operating engine-driven vehicles, and when George turned the controls over to him, he felt comfortable for the first time in that little boat.

After Steve made such a splash doing his own motorcycle stunts in the 1963 motion picture *The Great Escape*, he invited George to go riding out in the desert with him. He had several bikes, and he'd pick out the right one for

George. George was eager to go, and the next weekend they went out to Pearblossom, a small town in the Mojave Desert. There, George said, their roles were reversed: Steve was now in his element, and he and the motorcycle were one splendid animal. Steve not only had grace, he had guts. There was no hill, no dune, he wouldn't roar up, and, whenever possible, he would shoot off the top of them.

That excursion got George started in the sport. He bought dirt bikes for himself and for each of the boys. Nearly every weekend they'd put the bikes in a truck, grab their helmets and gloves, and head out to the desert. All of them loved desert riding, but Bryan was the most adventurous, the most like Steve McQueen.

One day, when George and Paul Newman were putting their company together, George took Paul out to the desert. Paul was good on a dirt bike—he had the right combination of guts and dexterity—but his real love was automobile racing, and he stayed with that.

George's roommate, fraternity brother, and doubles partner on the tennis team at UCLA, Kelly Clark, had gone on to Yale after UCLA. After finishing his year at Old Eli, he decided to enter divinity school, and then he became an Episcopalian minister. No one but Kelly Clark could possibly officiate at our wedding.

George and I were going to memorize our parts in the wedding ceremony. George had a problem with one part, where the minister says, "To be thy lawful, wedded wife till death do you part." George thought it should be "till death does you part." Since it's death that's doing the parting, the third-person singular should be used. I don't think he was all that serious about the grammar; it was really a manifestation of his nervousness.

As we were on the turnpike, en route to our nuptial ceremony in our 1937 Ford Phaeton, I looked down to memorize my words and to try to determine whether George had a point. I should have known better; it didn't take long before I had to throw up. George pulled to the side of the road, and I slid onto the grass and barfed my brains out, with cars whizzing behind me and George operatically singing "Here Comes the Bride."

The ceremony took place at a little church in North Haven, Connecticut, where Kelly was the rector. The wedding was charming. My parents and my sisters were there, and so were Mabel and Patsy; Jimmy Hammerstein, Oscar's son and one of our close friends; and Eddie Rissien, my longtime pal from Des Moines.

Kelly Clark was elegant, spiritual, and loving just as he is today. I couldn't have asked for a happier, more gentle, more human wedding experience. We had champagne in the rectory afterward, which added to our buoyancy. We laughed and cried and hugged. Then George and I and the little creature inside me got back in our comedy vehicle and returned to New York.

After the summer in East Rochester, we had taken an apartment in New York City, on the eighth floor of a building on West End Avenue and Seventy-ninth Street. One night, when I was eight months pregnant, we came home after dinner, pushed the button for the self-service elevator, and discovered the wretched thing was out of order. I thought I could walk up the eight flights if I rested at frequent intervals. George said, "No way," and he picked me up, me and the eight-month-old creature inside me, and carried me to the eighth floor. On the way I counted the steps. Each floor had twenty stairs, so we traversed a total of a hundred and sixty steps. I felt like he was Sir Walter Raleigh and I was Marie Antoinette, though I guess those two never knew each other.

On the night of October 3, 1953, George and I came home after having dinner with George's stepfather, Ken, and his wife, Bernadine. I was exhausted, and George had a headache, so we hit the sack right away. A couple of hours later, at 12:45 a.m., my water broke. I was excited. I thought, *Oh my gosh. I'm going to have a baby right on* schedule. I was due to give birth on October 3, and here it was just the beginning of the fourth. I was poised, I was both vibrant, and at peace, ready for the sacred event. George was not experiencing the same serenity; he was bustling around to be sure we were doing everything right.

I had polished my toenails. I had my little bag already packed, so we went downstairs, got in the Ford Phaeton, and, with the top up, started for the hospital. As we drove east on Eighty-sixth Street, I saw a White Castle hamburger joint and said, "George, let's stop here."

"You want a hamburger?" he asked, incredulous.

"Maybe two. I'm hungry."

"No, but, but, babe, aren't you supposed to not eat anything for six hours or a whole day before you have the baby?"

"It's okay. I'm hungry." In my mind was something Mama had once said to me. "Don't have a baby on Sunday without having any food in you." I don't know what kind of old wives' tale that might have been, but I was hungry, and my eyes were glistening for that hamburger.

George parked, and we went inside. White was the right name for the place: going through the door was like walking into a men's room. You were blasted by whiteness, no shadows. I downed my two hamburgers, we got back in the car and sped off to Doctors Hospital.

In those days, no one, not the husband or a family member, was allowed past the nurse's desk of the maternity ward. You said good-bye there and surrendered yourself to hospital protocols. It was so different from today, when your husband can not only be in the room, he can record the whole birth with a video camera.

I was taken into a huge labor room, with a lot of metal beds with high backs. It was empty and dark and horrible, I was the only one in it. I didn't know where anybody was, but finally, a nurse came in, and I started talking to her. I said I wanted a natural childbirth. Her response was, "Everything is going to be fine if you just shut up and push." When the labor pains hit me with full force, I said, "Just put me to sleep." And they did. I performed well. First, I delivered the hamburgers, then I delivered the baby.

Adam, our firstborn, joined the world at just past the seventh hour of the fourth day of October 1953. Some months before, we had decided that if our baby was a boy, we'd name him Adam. It had a good sound and Adam was the first male and we had high hopes for our boy so—Adam.

Almost exactly a year later, I was pregnant again. I was on my way to Hollywood to appear in my first film, a Mickey Spillane thriller called *Kiss Me Deadly*. I didn't have to test for the part or even read for it, as the producers had seen my work on television, and they wanted me. I adapted easily to film acting. I hardly noticed there was a difference, but one thing stood out. Even if you were acting in a small film, which this one was, you got treated more luxuriously than in the theater or in television. The hairdresser and wardrobe lady were always watching to see if they could be helpful, there was always coffee and something to eat nearby, and the whole atmosphere was businesslike but more relaxed.

At the time, George was directing an off-Broadway play at the Theatre de Lys and was working ten-hour days. Around 9:30 in the evening, he took me in a cab to the airport, and Adam and I got aboard our plane to California. This was before jets, so it was a long flight, but we had a berth and were warm and comfortable the whole flight.

When George got back to our apartment, he was involved in an incident. This is his description of what happened. As he got out of the cab on arriving home, he noticed two big men about to enter our apartment building. It was around midnight by this time, so their behavior looked suspicious. He went in the building, anyway, and they followed him inside. He pushed the button for the self-service elevator. When it came, he got in, and they pushed in right behind him. He hit the eight button, and one of them pushed the two button. When the interior door slid back on the second floor, one of the men pushed the outer door open and held it, then reached into his coat and pulled out a switch knife. The other man did the same, and the man who had exited the elevator got back in, grabbed George's wrist, and pressed the blade of his switch knife against the inside of George's wrist. The other man held his switch knife to George's neck.

"Now keep your mouth shut," one of them said in a very tense voice.

George later found out that there had been a police action uptown, a massive flushing out of drug dealers and addicts, who were now coming down to other areas to get money and find dealers. These two men were badly in need of a fix.

"Give me all you money, you watch, you jewelry, everything," said the man who was holding his knife to George's neck.

George took his money out of his pocket and undid his watch. The two men grabbed both, patted him down briefly, then ran out of the elevator, down the stairs to the first floor, and out of the building. Both elevator doors closed, and the elevator rose.

During the ascent to the eighth floor, George remembered reading an article by W. R. Smith, president of American Airlines. It said that when human beings are caught in a terrifying crisis, they experience the fight/

flight syndrome. They are impelled either to fight their way out of the situation or flee from it. In an airplane crisis, you can do neither. You have to stay in your seat, with your belt fastened, you have no control over what's going to happen. That thought lit George's mind. He'd been in the heart of a fight/flight situation in that elevator and could neither flee nor try to fight against the two men and their knives.

It was a cold night, and he was wearing the overcoat I loved so much. He walked into our apartment, didn't take his overcoat off, and sat down on the sofa. Our Doberman, Gaby, took her position beside him. There was one question in his mind: what would have happened if Adam and I had been in that elevator with him? The thought gripped him; he sat for the next six hours, virtually without moving, imagining the awful things that could have happened if I'd been there. At a little after 7:00 a.m., he called the police. They came and showed him some mug shots, and one said, "You were lucky. Usually, they stick the knife in your throat, then find out if you've got any money."

When the police left, George called me. He didn't want me to know what had happened, but he did want to plant the idea in my head that we should move. He started casually. He said, "I've been thinking. Now that we've got one child and another one on the way, we should probably be in a better neighborhood."

Mabel and I had just walked in from the airport, and the strangeness of his bringing up this subject at this time hit me right away. It didn't take me long to get the story of the attack out of him. It was shocking, and we agreed that as soon as his play opened, he should look for a new apartment.

Two days later I called him. "Have you found a new place yet?" I asked.

"Not yet. Couple of things I had to do first," he said.

"Well, don't look anymore. I've found a little house two doors up from Muth's, and I put a down payment on it. It's time for us to be in California."

That was the way and that was the day the decision to move west was made.

Motherhood, Grandmotherhood, Great-Grandmotherhood And Boyz 'n' The Hood

I'm pausing. To let myself be invaded, to let the children and the dogs I've loved and the family I've had and lost enter the room. When you are well into telling your life story, you see what a folly you've become part of. There's not enough time and space in which to set the whole thing down or even a fraction of it. The jumble of things you've done would fill a thousand hard disks. Memories are the unruly things. They steal silently in on cat feet and lie in the sun by the window, not acknowledging you're in the room also. And when you want to fondle them, to be closer to the him or her who is in the memory, just as silently they slip away.

Memories bring back another time, another you. The recall of a show you were on that you hadn't thought about in years transforms you into the ingenue you were then. You think, *I ought to call Paul Lynde and ask how much of those days at Northwestern he remembers* . . . Then you realize he's been dead for a quarter of a century, and probably so is everyone else who was at Northwestern. You remember how deeply, deeply saddened you were when you heard that Paul had died.

So I am putting the concept of organization away and am going to let moods and feelings come to me in whatever shapes and colors they wear. The mood I'm most comfortable with is when I think of my family. I could have lived without being an actress, but I could never have made it through this life without having the children, grandchildren, and great-grandchild that now fill this stage of my life.

Here are parts and pieces of our family life, those that come softly with smiles, those that come sadly with regrets. They assemble around me this night, and while they're here, I will tell of them.

As soon as we moved to California, I began working regularly. George was staging nightclub acts in Las Vegas. It wasn't the part of the entertainment industry he wanted to pursue, but he had run into Howard Keel in Scotland when Keel was performing his one-man show there. Keel had asked George what he thought of it, and George had said it was good, that there was no question that Howard could sing, that he had a magnificent voice, but that there were parts of the show he felt could be better. Keel asked him to stay in Glasgow and make the improvements he saw.

The next day George began rehearsals, and at the end of a week, Keel was getting standing ovations. George shaped the act again when Keel played the Copacabana in

New York and again when he went to the Sands Hotel in Las Vegas.

John Williams, who would later become principal conductor of the Boston Pops and would write many famous movie scores, including those for *Star Wars*, *Superman*, and *Harry Potter*, and the theme music for four Olympic Games, was Keel's accompanist. He and George started out in the Vegas acts business together.

When George did Jeff Chandler's Vegas act, Henry Mancini, who would later become as famous a movie composer as John Williams, was the accompanist. Sammy Cahn, the great lyricist, loved George and wrote special material for several of the acts George was creating. After Keel came Eddie Fisher, who was then a big star, and after him, Dean Martin. All were successful, and Eddie asked George to produce his upcoming television series, *The Eddie Fisher Show*. George did.

A huge imbroglio followed. In the middle of the season, Eddie left his wife, Debbie Reynolds, and took up with Liz Taylor. One night before it was out in the open, we were at Debbie and Eddie's house for dinner. After the meal Debbie and I were in the living room having a musical session. I at the piano, she playing her French horn. Liz and Eddie were in the next room, at the beginning of their love affair. It was huge news when it broke, since Eddie and Debbie were the perfect young couple, with two charming children.

The paparazzi chased Eddie and Liz everywhere, while heartbroken Debbie was showing her pluck by giving interviews outside her front door. The question was, what was

Eddie going to do? Stay married like a good boy or, the unthinkable, leave Debbie and run off with alluring Liz? No one needed to know more than George, who was producing *The Eddie Fisher Show* for television.

While we were at dinner one night, Eddie called George and said he'd decided that he was going to be with Liz. That produced a whole new set of circumstances, and George was sucked into the vortex. He, Warren Cowan, Liz's publicist, and Eddie had a summit meeting at Liz's house. She was in bed, suffering from the strain, but at the same time, it seemed to George, enjoying the tumult she was causing. She'd been cast as the villainess because she'd broken up a little nest, but she was showing that great beauty could also have great heart, and she deeply regretted the pain Debbie was feeling. However, Eddie was now her man, and nothing was going to change that.

To evade the paparazzi and the clamor, Eddie went to New York. He found no peace there, so he came back to LA. The children and I were going to be away, so George suggested Eddie could stay at our house. Eddie grabbed the offer.

One of Eddie's major hits was a song called "Oh! My Papa," which tells of a Jewish grandfather who means everything to the boy singing. As it happened, George's Jewish grandfather was staying at our house; he was the perfect late-night companion for Eddie. While all the newspapers and magazines and television crews were searching for Eddie Fisher, he was hunkered down, out of sight, and comfortable and cozy at our house, with his surrogate grandfather, Alex Erlich. George would come home after dinner and find Eddie and Pa having a glass of wine and talking a little Yiddish.

Our social life was burgeoning. We were out many nights dining with the Howard Keels; the Sammy Cahns; Kirk and Anne Douglas; Lou Calhern; Rouben Mamoulian, one of the industry's top directors; Dinah Shore; and Paul Newman and Joanne Woodward.

We saw a lot of the Newmans. I did two pictures with Paul: *The Rack*, which was my first film after *Kiss Me Deadly*, then *Butch Cassidy and the Sundance Kid*. Our boys grew up parallel to the Newmans' three girls, Nell, Lissy, and Clea, so that brought us together often, too. I have to stop. . . .

Paul died last week. It's time to pull over, shut off the engine, and think about what his passing means. Paul was royal, no question. He wouldn't say so. He didn't do things self-consciously to get applause, to get noticed. He just went about being one of the best actors of all time and one of the kindest men of his century.

In 1971, Paul was directing and starring in a film with Henry Fonda and Lee Remick, *Sometimes a Great Notion*. It was being shot in Bend, Oregon. Paul and Joanne invited me and our kids to come up and spend some time with them and their kids. They sent a private jet for us. I remember the landing. All we could see were green trees; we were practically touching the treetops before the runway appeared.

We stayed in a beautiful house on an exclusive beach. My son Georgie was the same age as their oldest daughter, Nell, and their other two daughters, Lissy and Clea, fit perfectly with Morgan and Dinah. It was a memorable time, not because anything spectacular happened, but because of the quality of life we shared. Paul knew how to do that, to enjoy life whenever the opportunity was there.

We and the Newmans shared parallel tragedies—the death of Paul's son Scott and the death of our son Bryan, both from drugs.

Paul and I shared acting experiences that were inventive and fun. In *Butch Cassidy and the Sundance Kid*, I was cast as the lady of the evening. To prepare for the role, I asked myself why Butch Cassidy would choose me out of all the lovelies in the cathouse. I went to the wig department and picked out a beautiful blond one that fell all the way down to my knees. Then I thought, *What's the best way to use this wig?* So, in the scene I got on top of Paul while he was lying on his bed. I let my long hair fall on him, and I sang a song to him because he had such beautiful blue eyes. I sang "Mighty Like a Rose" softly into his ear. It's a favorite scene of mine.

In 1972 Paul and George formed a company together because both of them wanted not only to produce films but to explore activities outside the industry. George brought in Bill Kimpton as their business adviser. Kimpton was head of Lehman Brothers in San Francisco at the time and later started Kimpton Hotels, which now range across the country. Both Paul and George invested in Kimpton Hotels, and those investments have proved to be very wise. Sargent Shriver and his Washington firm became their legal counsel.

George produced a TV film for the company titled *See How She Runs* (1978). It starred Paul's wife, Joanne Wood-

ward, and she won the Emmy that year for best performance by an actress.

Of the three film projects Paul and George assembled
for development, I thought the most interesting was one
based on a novel called *The Front Runner*, by Patricia Nell
Warren, which was published in 1974. It is the story of
America's best mile runner and a big hopeful for a gold
medal in the Olympics. As the young hero approaches
world record time and becomes more and more of a
celebrity, word seeps out that he is in a gay relationship
with his coach. That puts the country in a difficult position. Its champion miler, its red, white, and blue athlete,
its potential world-record holder is gay?

Paul was to play the coach, which immediately stirred
controversy. How would appearing in this role affect his
career? Would it impinge on the handsome hero figure he
had so indelibly created? Would it damage his star status,
or would he be considered innovative and courageous for
taking on such a role? Ultimately, the studio decided that
investing in the film was too dangerous, and the project
was canceled. Through the years Paul and George talked
about what would have happened if they'd made that film.
The idea of exploring new frontiers was at the heart of
their company's aspirations.

I have a host of other moments and memories about
Paul in my mind, but this doesn't feel like the time to
bring them out and shake them out. I'm sitting outside
tonight and there's a soft wind blowing and I think I'll just
let my thoughts about Paul float on it. The last thought I
have is of the lines near the end of *Hamlet*, when Hamlet

has died, and Horatio says about him: "Let four captains bear Hamlet like a soldier to the stage, for he was likely, had he been put on, to have proved most royal."

Paul was put on the stage of life, and in his walk across it, he did indeed prove, in all the ways a man can, he was most royal.

The heart of our social life was spent with Sydney Chaplin and his then-girlfriend, Joan Collins. In those days, Sydney was living at Gene Kelly's house on Rodeo Drive in Beverly Hills; he introduced us to Gene and his wife, actress Betsy Blair. From the start, we were friends. Gene loved to play two-man volleyball, so much so that he'd built a court behind his house. George was highly adept from his years of playing the game at State Beach in Santa Monica, so a special bond was formed between them. That bond grew through the years; when Gene got married for the second time, in 1960, he asked George to be his best man.

George was gone a lot, working out the locations for his pictures, sometimes for weeks at a time. So I'd be alone with the housekeeper and the children. When George came home, often he couldn't understand why things we'd agreed to hadn't been done and why others, to his surprise, had been done. He wondered why the children seemed unkempt and, in a way, uncared for. Yes, if there was one giant source of stress between us, it was, and I'm sure always will be, how the children should be raised. George feels our disagreement about it was what kept us separated so much of the time.

I was brought up by Mama. Daddy left everything about

raising us girls to her, and she was loving and encouraged us always to be free spirits. That's what I brought to my children.

Our little house on Beverly Glen Boulevard was two doors away from Mabel's house, so we saw her almost every day. When she and George talked about what he should be doing, she was consistent in saying he was too impatient, he should get a job in television as a stage manager and work his way up from there. His response was, "Muth, I've done that. I did my apprenticeship in New York. I don't want to be a stage manager. I want to be a producer and director."

I wrote earlier about the night George and Marlon Brando met and how they became friends. It was true. Almost every evening, when George came home from scouting the city, Marlon was there, waiting for him. A few months after they met, Marlon started his own independent production company, Pennebaker, Inc., named after his mother, Dorothy Pennebaker. One night, when he and George went out to dinner, Marlon said he'd thought a lot about what he was going to say, and now he was sure he was right, he asked George to run the company.

Typical of the way they kidded each other, George said, "That's really good of you, Mar, but I'm pretty tied up these days. I've got to be at Unemployment at ten tomorrow morning. That kind of thing."

"Yeah," Marlon laughed, "and you'll be working on your baseball card collection. I know how it is."

Then they talked in earnest about what an exciting prospect it would be. Marlon said he'd made his father president of the company, and he wanted George to meet him. "It's just a formality," Marlon explained. "I wanted to give my father a position, but that's what it is. A position. He won't run things. You will."

The next morning, when George and I had breakfast with Mabel, she asked him how his employment possibilities were coming along.

"Not too bad, not too bad," he said.

"Any news about anything?" Mabel queried.

"It's looking a little better about getting the play I optioned produced at the Pasadena Playhouse. I think that could happen."

"That's it?"

"Pretty much . . . Well, I'd better get back to the house. Got some phone calls to make." He got up and headed to the door, turned back, and added, "There is one other possibility. I hesitate to talk about it because you feel so strongly that I should be getting a job as a stage manager, and this isn't that."

"I've suggested it. It's the best I can come up with, but it's your life. You have to do what you think is best for you," said Mabel. "Tell me. What's this other possibility?"

With a smile, George said, "Actually, it's more than a possibility, Muth. I'm going to run Marlon Brando's production company."

That was the only time I ever saw Mabel flabbergasted. It took her a while to grasp both the fact and the implications of what George had said.

During our first years in Los Angeles, life was busy.

George was running Marlon's company; I had to look after three little boys, born eighteen months apart, and I'd begun playing the mother on the television series *Lassie*. I thought this would be the perfect arrangement: I'd be playing a mother on television, and my acting life would be very much like my home life.

Wrong. I had to be on the set every morning at 6:30, the production was tightly organized. And the show wasn't really about our little television family; it was about the real star, the dog. He or she, there were several interchangeable collies, got the attention and care. Still, it was enjoyable. I love being a mother, even that mother. I loved every part of it, all that it entailed, and still do.

Just after *Lassie*, I remember standing up at the end of a long day, pausing for a minute, and thinking, *"My God, I'm upright. What an interesting condition."* Another time I was bending over Adam and putting little pants on him. I was shoving them up his legs when he jumped to help and smashed into my chin, causing me to bite deeply into my tongue. Poor little thing. He was so worried, and I had to reassure him that I was all right, trying to sound normal with this frankfurter in my mouth.

Adam was calm and happy as a little boy; Bryan was not quite the same. By the time he was four months old, he had four teeth, way ahead of schedule, and that caused him great discomfort. Also, he slept in the crib in our room, and George and I would have long talks about parenting. They weren't fights exactly, but I really didn't want to have those heavy discussions about how we should raise the children. I don't know if Bryan was aware of our conversations and, if he was, how much he might have been affected by them.

I enjoyed doing *Lassie*. I was a mother at home and a mother at work, and for me, nothing could be better. But the sands of life were starting to shift again. Syd and Joan's relationship was wearing out, and George and I were having a conflict about the same old thing, how the children should be raised. And, as I would soon find out, Joan had eyes for George. Though I didn't know it at the time, I was about to begin the most difficult period of my life.

After I left *Lassie*, and being a bit in despair about things between George and me, and not knowing what was going on with Joan Collins, I took the boys and went to visit my sister Mary in Darien, Connecticut. I was concerned about the boys, who were now aged one and a half, three, and four and a half. Adam was squinting his eyes a lot, and I didn't know why, and Bryan, who was three, was frequently saying, "No, no." I realized later it was because Pa, who was staying with us at the time, would give a piece of gum to Adam and Georgie, but for some reason, he wouldn't give one to Bryan.

Life was pleasant in Darien. Mary was married to Bob Castle, a vice president of the J. Walter Thompson Company, an advertising agency in New York. They welcomed my boys, and Bob was a loving surrogate father. Life was so appealing, I bought a little house nearby for fifteen thousand dollars, and the boys and I moved in. It was a two-story home on a rather large plot of land, and for another $150, I totally refurbished the house.

George was in New York, and he came to Darien for a visit. He stayed one night, and I got pregnant. Not long after that, I got a call to come and do a television show in Los Angeles. I had to take off immediately. It was difficult because all three of the boys had the flu. George, who was still in New York, said he would pick them up and bring them back to Los Angeles.

In the making of the television show, I had to run, jump, turn around, and run back again. We rehearsed it over and over. It was exhausting, and in my condition, unwise. Soon I started staining. That was on a Friday. On Sunday I started bleeding; every five minutes something akin to a large liver came out of me. George took me to the hospital. I had a miscarriage.

I was deeply, emotionally affected, heartbroken. I came home on Wednesday, anemic and basically a wreck. That night I got a call from New York. They wanted me to replace an actress in a show that was out of town and heading for Broadway. I told George I thought I should do it. Mabel said she'd help in every way she could, especially by looking after the children. George was what he always has been to me, loving and caring. He said if I wanted to do the play, he would support me in every way.

I got on a plane, went east, and joined the production. We stayed out of town an extra week, then opened on Broadway. We closed the night we opened. The next night I went to Sardi's alone for dinner. Robert Whitehead, the famous producer, and Harold Clurman, the famous director, were also dining there. They invited me to their table, and I went over. They had something in mind. They wanted me to replace an actress in the Broadway play *A Touch of the Poet*, which starred Helen Hayes. It would be a four-month commitment. That was stunning news. Since I was all set to go back to LA, I said I'd have to think about it, and I would let them know tomorrow.

Right after I got back to the hotel, George called. There was an urgency in his voice, "Babe," he said, "you have to come back. The children need you." Then I told him about the offer to be in *A Touch of the Poet* and that I thought I should do it. Once again, he was totally support-ive. He told me not to worry, and assured me that if I wanted to do the play, he would take care of everything out there.

I went to Darien and spent the weekend with Mary and Bob. I was terribly worn out, and when I got back to New York and stepped off the train at Grand Central Station, I broke down in tears. But I learned my role and joined the cast of *A Touch of the Poet*.

In the ensuing weeks, my health didn't improve. I was anemic and sad and lifeless. It would take me two hours to get myself together to leave the theater every night. One night when I got back to the hotel, I called George and told him how terribly I missed everybody, and that I spe-cially needed to see the children. He was understanding, and he said he would send the children to me or bring them.

I was grateful to him, but I said, "No, at least not yet. I don't think I'm up to handling them right now. Let's go day by day and see if things improve."

He said, "Okay, but be calm. We'll do what's best for you."

Two nights later I was standing in the wings, about to make my entrance, when I looked down and saw the newspaper Helen Hayes had been reading. The headline was JOAN COLLINS SHOULD GET AN OSCAR FOR THE LOVE SCENE SHE PLAYED WITH GEORGE ENGLUND LAST NIGHT. How does something like that affect you? You stand in my place, and try to remember what you're supposed to say when you get onstage after just having seen that headline. I had a blank look and weaved a bit, but I got through the scene.

Three nights later, at almost exactly 4:00 a.m., the phone rang. It seemed louder than I'd never heard a phone ring before, it shattered my sleep and the night silence. When I picked up the phone and said hello, Joan Collins's voice greeted me.

"Cloris, this is Joan," she said, as if I wouldn't immediately identify that English accent. "George just left here. We see each other every day. I'm in love with him. What do you want to do about that?"

I was sleepy and disoriented. "I don't know," I said. "I'm not sure what the choices are. Do you think you two can make a go of it?"

"Yes, I do. I love him. I absolutely love him, but"—she was becoming very emotional—"he loves you. Oh God . . . I have to go."

She didn't even have time to hang the phone up. She dropped it and ran to the bathroom. I could hear her throwing up. I guess the poor girl had been drinking.

When I told George about the call, he was angry that Joan had made it. We didn't really discuss what was going on between him and her, but whatever it was, his major concern was my stability and that of the family.

I finally finished my work in *A Touch of the Poet* and went back to LA. I was in a very reduced state. I didn't know what the state of my marriage was. I felt simply awful that I'd been away from my children so long, and physically, I was still very anemic. When I arrived at the airport in Los Angeles, George and the boys were waiting for me. What I saw was a sad, curious group.

Adam was off by himself, fifteen feet away from the others. He was looking down, his eyes hooded. Bryan was standing beside George, and George was holding baby George in his arms. Little George kept saying, "Where's Mama? Where's Mama?" He was looking right at me and didn't know I was his mother.

We went home, and as soon as we entered the house, Bryan led me to a rocking chair and had me sit in it. Then he climbed into my lap, and we sat there, rocking together. After a while he said, "Are you really my mother?" That was the saddest day of my life. It would take a long time to climb out of that somberness.

Before I'd gone to New York, we'd moved from the little house on Beverly Glen, next to Mabel, to one on Comstock Avenue in West Los Angeles. That lasted a year, and then George and I separated. He moved to an English cottage above the Sunset Strip. He was working hard to get the film *The Ugly American* made. Finally, Universal Pictures green-lighted it, and he was going to produce and direct a major motion picture based on a best-selling book and starring Marlon Brando.

This was everything he'd been working for, but almost more important to him was that the boys go along with him to Thailand, where *The Ugly American* would be shot. He felt it was crucial for them to experience different countries and different cultures, and he believed that this would be a perfect opportunity. There was a problem, though, and it was evident right away. Somebody would have to go along to take care of the boys. George and I had discussions about it, and ultimately, we faced the obvious. I was the best one to go. We made a pact that under no circumstances would we fight during this trip. We both understood the responsibilities he'd been bearing as a producer and first-time director, and we realized that an awesome opportunity lay before him.

We had the experience of a lifetime. I have pictures of the boys and me with Buddhist monks and in temples and kickboxing gyms and outdoor markets on the river. We visited fascinating places all over Bangkok. Every morning we'd leave the hotel in a *samlor*, a three-wheeled pedicab peddled by an always happy Thai young man, and explore the city.

Also, I must say, and George agrees, I took excellent care of George. I brought him juice when he was shooting outside and the temperature was ninety-seven degrees and the humidity was 97 percent. In his words, I was "an outstanding wife and a wonderful companion throughout the whole adventure." The fact that we had promised that we absolutely would not fight brought a kind of magic. There was not one moment of conflict the whole time we were there. Sometime before, while he was on a six-week location scout, he'd broken off with Joan Collins, and she had taken up with Warren Beatty.

When we got home, we were both enthusiastic about being a family again. We found an appealing house in Brentwood Park, bought it, and moved in. We had a lively social life there, not only with industry folk, but with people from the State Department and the Rand Corporation, and people related to the production and postproduction of *The Ugly American*. It was during this time that our fourth son, Morgan, was born.

While our house was excellent in all ways, there was an especially grand one two blocks away, a Southern mansion built by Pat O'Brien, a movie star of the thirties, forties, and fifties. The address was 196 South Rockingham. O'Brien called it Tara because it was an almost exact replica of the estate in *Gone with the Wind*. We couldn't afford the house, and Pat O'Brien wasn't actually ready to sell it, but George thought we had to have it. There were five large bedrooms. Well, you couldn't call them bedrooms. They were really suites, and thus each child would have what amounted to his own apartment. Finally, George worked out a deal that Pat O'Brien accepted, and now we owned Tara.

What an adventure it was to move in. The house was more beautiful than we'd realized before we'd owned it. There was a sweeping staircase to the second floor; a handsome, tasteful living room; and a large library with a bay window looking out onto the extensive backyard. It also had an attic that could have been turned into a third floor. The servants quarters had two bedrooms and a living room. The guesthouse, in the back of the property, had a large, beautifully proportioned bedroom, a billiard room, and a sauna.

George and I sped around, looking for the things we needed for the house. We had to buy what seemed like two acres of carpet, new drapes, and new outside furniture to go around the huge swimming pool.

Shortly after we had settled in, our business manager called me and said, "Cloris, I've got a bill here for thirteen toilet seats. Is that correct? What are you doing over there?"

I said, "Eddie, this was hard for me to believe, too. There are thirteen bathrooms in this place. And just between you and me, I'm going to do number one and number two in every one of them."

In the early days at Rockingham, we had it all—a glorious home, beautiful kids, and flourishing careers. I think sometimes we humans don't take proper notice when things are going really well. There's no doubt in anybody's mind when things are bad. After all, the problem is right in front of you. However, when everything is all right, and the world's in harmony, we don't just stop and notice how good things are. I have seen over and over, this tendency to impregnate the current hour with thoughts about what dark things might happen in the next one.

While we were in the Rockingham house, our fifth child, and our first girl, was born. As my due date approached, I thought I was going into labor, so I went to the hospital. I stayed there all night, and nothing developed, so I went home. Three days later, my water broke. I was glad, because it meant I'd have my daughter on a Sunday morning. We went to St. John's Hospital, and they put me in the labor room, which was quite different from the one in New York. It was beautiful and welcoming. I was feeling fine, but my doctor couldn't check on me, because he was very busy helping another doctor with triplets down the hall. With all the instruments being gathered, all the cursing, and all the moving, it was like a factory. Sadly, despite the herculean efforts, all three triplets died.

I kept saying, "I want to go into the delivery room." I didn't know why I kept saying it. I wasn't actually thinking I should be in the delivery room, but my mouth kept saying it. The nurses weren't sure what to do, so they got word to the doctor, and he gave them the go-ahead to put me in the delivery room. In the delivery room, I felt happy. I couldn't say why; I just felt I was where I should be.

The doctor came in, examined me, and immediately went to work performing a cesarean section. I didn't know it then, but just about everything that could be wrong was wrong. The baby was turned completely the wrong way, and her umbilical cord was wrapped around her, posing a grave threat. The doctor was looking at a frightening picture. After doing the emergency surgery, he came out and said to George, "I think we can save Cloris, but I'm not sure about the baby." I didn't know any of that at the time.

When I went to see the doctor for my six-week checkup,

we were in the room together, and he burst into tears. He told me what good fortune it was that I had been in the delivery room early. Normally, it takes twenty minutes to do a cesarean section, but because I was already on the operating table, he was able to do it in just about five minutes, even though he had to cut me from my navel all the way down to get the baby out. So that voice inside me that had kept saying, *I want to be in the delivery room,* had saved my life and Dinah's.

We took a long, thoughtful time to find a name for our baby girl. George felt it was a good idea to look at our kids before we named them, to know them for a few months, and see which name might fit. After two months, he proposed that we call our daughter Cheyenne. It had a lovely lilt he said. Cheyenne Englund. It was different from other girls' names, as she was different and unique. He offered the thought at dinner, and Mabel and I right away gave it the raspberry.

"Cheyenne? You've got to be kidding," one of us snorted.

"If you want to go that route, why not Pocahontas or albino squaw with long umbilicus?" the other joked. We howled.

George thought the idea deserved a little more consideration but ultimately accepted defeat. He told Marlon about the stony lack of enthusiasm for his suggestion. Marlon had a different response, though he didn't tell George about it. Later, when his daughter was born, he named her Cheyenne.

We chose Dinah. The name seemed to rest gently on our baby girl and to embody the promise suggested by her tiny form. Sometime in the following week—I think it was five days later—we gave a dinner party, and Dinah Shore was among the guests. She wanted to see the new baby, so we brought her to the crib, and she oohed and aahed about how beautiful she was.

"What's her name?" she asked as she leaned over the baby.

"Dinah," I said. Then I thought, *Oh, oh.*

Dinah Shore turned to us, emotion visible on her face. "You named her after me?" There was a tremble in her voice.

The truth was, we hadn't thought of Dinah Shore or anybody else while we cruised around for a name. Some very fast footwork was called for.

"Yes," I said, my eyes mirroring the emotion in hers. "George and I thought you were the perfect role model for our baby."

I mean, what could I do? She was having something close to a religious experience. I couldn't slap my forehead and say, "Can you believe it? We never once thought of you when we picked the name."

Our next international excursion, a few years later, was to Italy, where George was producing *The Shoes of the Fisherman* a film based on the 1963 best-selling novel of the same name by Morris West. It would star Anthony Quinn, Laurence Olivier, Oskar Werner, and a fine supporting cast. Before principal photography started, George took Bryan on a trip with him. When they came back, George described their adventure.

Bryan was mad about go-karts, so George found a major go-kart track outside Rome. They had a specially built model they called *il Vulcano*, the Volcano. The first morning they were in Rome, they went to the track where *il Vulcano* stood waiting for Bryan. This machine was far more powerful than anything Bryan had ever driven.

Our lad was fearless: he put on his helmet and goggles, got in, and started around the track. When he hit the accelerator, the thing bucked off the pavement and sent him spinning into a series of doughnuts. Bryan was looking down the muzzle of a real challenge, and he stayed with it. He stayed on the course till it was time for lunch. The next morning George asked Bryan if he wanted to go to the go-kart track again.

It was a surprise when Bryan said, "No, I'd like to see why you think this place is so great."

"All right," George said, and they went downstairs, got into their car, and drove to the Vatican.

They paid a visit to Michelangelo's sculpture the *Pietà*, which in those days stood by itself, with no barrier before it. You could walk right up and stand in front of it. The *Pietà* portrays Mary holding her dead son Jesus after he's been crucified. George and Bryan moved up close to the sculpture. Bryan stood in front of George, and George wrapped his arms around Bryan.

"This is, to me, the most beautiful thing ever created by man," George said as they surveyed the enormous sculpture. "Imagine, it was carved out of one huge, raw piece of marble. See the folds in Mary's gown, the imprint of her hand on her dead son's back. Can you see the unmea-surable sadness in her eyes?"

Beneath George's hands, Bryan's stomach muscles contracted. He'd started to cry. That made George cry, so they stood there, father and son, before the majesty of the *Pietà,* tears streaming down their faces.

"Imagine," George whispered through the emotion, "Michelangelo was only twenty-three when he created this."

Later, as they sat outdoors at a bistro, having lunch, Bryan was on fire. He wanted to learn to sculpt. "Excellent," George said, joyous over Bryan's response. After lunch he went out and found a maestro, Lodovico Sabatini, a won-derful man, an illustrious teacher. George and Bryan were staying at the Hilton Hotel atop Monte Mario, and from their balcony, they could look out over the whole city of Rome. Every afternoon, when George came back from his work, Bryan and Lodovico would be out on the balcony, in the timeless pose of teacher and student.

"Disegna! Disegna!" Lodovico would call out to Bryan. "Draw! Draw!" He wanted to free Bryan's hand, so he had him make large circles on a huge drawing pad. Bryan re-sponded with all the young boy's determination in him. It was a moment of pure poetry for his father.

When production started, our whole family moved to Rome. We found a perfect apartment in an old building above a piazza where fresh flowers were sold each day. The boys went to the American School in Rome and had a whole new experience there.

While in Italy, we took a ski holiday. It was the first

time the boys and I visited the mountains of Italy. As young boys do, they picked up the sport easily and were never off the slopes.

George had to leave early, and after he'd gone, I fell while I was trying out my new ski technique and broke my leg. It was the worst kind of break, a spiral fracture. I had to be taken back to Rome in an ambulance. Either the ambulance drivers didn't know how badly injured I was and that I needed immediate attention or they were simply following Italian custom when they stopped for a relaxing lunch. The pain in my leg wasn't tolerable, but there was nothing I could do. There would be no relief until I got to Rome.

I still feel the vestigial effects of that injury, but they are overshadowed by memories of the way of life we were part of during our time in Italy: the wine, the phenomenal Italian meals, the exceptional people we met and worked with, and above all, the pleasure of living in Rome. One of my memories is of Dinah, aged two, arguing very much in the Italian way—arms gesturing, eyes alive—with her nanny— in Italian. She must have been vaccinated by that experience; later, when she had grown up, she lived in Sicily for a year.

There were other adventures abroad. In 1967 George was making *Dark of the Sun* in Africa, a controversial film about mercenaries in a war in the Congo in the 1960s, so he had to scout the east, west and south of the continent. On one of those scouting trips, he took Adam so they could share an adventure together. The pilot of their scouting plane let Adam, who was fifteen at the time, take over the controls for long periods. George told me how he'd wake up and find they were in a steep climb, Adam lazily taking them up the face of a beautiful cloud, then descending on the other side.

One night, they were stuck in Mau Mau country. The Mau Mau were the most ferocious raiders on the continent, and nobody went into Mau Mau territory without police or military accompaniment. George felt he had to see these "badlands" and, after considerable talks with the authorities, decided it would be safe if they were out of the area before dark.

He, Adam, the writer who had accompanied them, and the driver were going down a dirt road at about sixty-five hundred feet on the back side of a mountain in the middle of Mau Mau country when a raging monsoon rain came pouring down. In George's mind was the police admonition that they absolutely had to reach a town at the bottom of that valley before dark. If they didn't, they would be out of contact, no one would know where they were, and they'd be vulnerable to attack by the Mau Mau.

The awesome deluge swiftly turned the road to mud, making it difficult to drive on. George and the writer would get behind the car and lift the back end to try to get it moving down the mountain. It was brutal work. Frequently the car slipped close to the edge of the road, and they were looking at a six-thousand-foot drop. Sometimes they just got back in the car and sat till they felt strong enough to try again.

Night came. Adam said it brought a kind of darkness he had never seen before. Untarnished by city lights, the great bowl of night sky filled them with a feeling of reverence. Planets and stars were arrayed in a way neither Adam nor George had ever seen. They felt like the Magi, that there was some message in all that glitter and blackness they were meant to decipher. They could not stop looking; they could not stop murmuring about the panorama above them.

But they had to keep moving. They had to get down the mountain. As they tried once again to move the car, they looked up and saw a line of Mau Mau on the embankment, looking down on them, silent, impassive. This could have meant the end of their lives, but the Mau Mau stood motionless, their spears beside them.

Adam said he wasn't frightened. Among the stoic Mau Mau observing them was a girl who was probably about Adam's age. Upon noticing each other, Adam and the girl exchanged appraising looks, then a few smiles. Then Adam moved closer to where she was standing. They seemed oblivious to the tension surrounding them. Using low sounds and sign language, they began to communicate. Had it not been for the highly charged circumstances, George felt that this could have been the beginning of a unique, life-long relationship.

In the early morning, at around two or three o'clock, the monsoon abated and the dirt road began to harden. A bit after dawn, they pulled into a tiny village with a tiny hostel, which had kept the lights on for them all night. The African proprietress said they had been terribly worried, but there was nothing they could have done in the middle of night. They were about to call the police to have them mount a search. The three of them were quite a sight. Adam brought back pictures of them covered from head to toe in red mud.

The subject of the film *Dark of the Sun*, turned out to be just too volatile, and it was clear that the film could not be safely produced in Africa, so George moved the production to Jamaica. And once again, the family went to live in a different culture. Jamaica appeals to every one of the senses, with its coffee, reggae music, dancing, and fresh fruits. Ian Fleming, author of the James Bond novels, had the perfect island residence in Jamaica. It was secluded, spacious, and open to the mountains on one side, and it had its own private cove below. We rented it.

Jim Brown, the Hall of Fame football player, was one of the stars of the picture. He was a private man, one who was reserved about forming friendships, but he was wonderful with the boys. He taught them a lot about football, especially about how to fire out of the backfield the moment the ball has been snapped.

The boys had an English tutor, a kind, gentle man who, I think, was more used to prim Eton types than boisterous American boys. He didn't seem to have the athletic ability to keep up with our three athletes and explorers, who were in the ocean a lot, snorkeling, skin-diving, and water-skiing. It was pretty much a boy's paradise.

The picture had the endorsement and participation of the Jamaica Defence Force, so we took many trips around the island in their aircraft. George also had a helicopter, which he used to get back and forth to scout locations and to reach the filming sites. He took the boys and me with him as often as possible.

One day we had particular need of the helicopter. Morgan suddenly became ill. We didn't know what it was, only that he was terribly sick. We flew him in the helicopter to the hospital in Kingston. On first examination, the doctors said it looked like a spinal problem, possibly meningitis. That was frightening news.

I remember so well how George and I sat in the sunlit courtyard of the hospital, waiting to hear the diagnosis. We wondered how we would feel, how we would handle the situation if it turned out that Morgan had spinal meningitis. Fortunately, and miraculously, it wasn't meningitis. It was mononucleosis, a far less worrisome illness.

Jamaica got into our souls, and every time we hear that reggae beat, we start to swing to it.

An Unbearable Sadness

I haven't really talked about him or his death. I've written his name and told anecdotes about him. That's all, and that's mainly because, after all the drama, the pain, the incomprehensibility of it, I don't know that I have anything coherent to say. I'll try. I'll start with the basic words.

Doper, stoner, junkie, crackhead—Bryan became those.

Six foot one, handsome, charming, and when he talked to you, it was like he was doing a soft-shoe. Brave. Loyal. Bryan was those.

When your son is an addict, when the fact can no longer be concealed—he nods off at dinner; he's gone most of the day, and you don't know where he is; and when you ask him where he's been and why he's so tired all the time, he tells you, "Don't get all weird, Mom. I just had a couple of beers"—when you hear all that and you look into the eyes of the son you brought into this world and see the unchallengeable certification of his addiction, you haven't heard or seen the worst part, namely, that you are more of an addict than he is.

You use only one drug, but it's got higher lethality than all of his combined. Your drug is hope, and you won't, you can't, you don't know how to give it up. Not today, not tomorrow, not ever will you give up your drug. You'll cling to it, hoard it, hide it, slide it out of sight, bring it out at night, because if you ever went to your stash and took that load of hope out and incinerated it, you'd be staring at the fact that your son is going to die. So you will never let go of that dirty, immolating drug you carry with you every day and everywhere, your hope.

You'll go through stages. First stage, you know he's a drug addict, but you hope it's not permanent, you hope he'll see what he's doing and quit, you hope somebody will talk sense into him, you hope he'll get counseling, you hope, most of all, he knows you love him. That alone should get him to stop. And you don't know, you don't want to know, that this hope you can't quit using is sending both of you down the road to hell.

Second stage is when he's been busted three times, when he's been in jail four nights in a row, when you get calls from a male voice you don't know, with an accent you can't fathom, who says you have to come and get Bryan. "He's in a room in a flophouse in Venice by himself. He is in really bad shape, ma'am. Somebody got to come and get him."

You know how bad my hope addiction was, is? I still hope Bryan's going to come back to me. The other day I was lying in bed, and my son Morgan came in. There was a shadow on the side of his face, and I sat up, because my God, he looked exactly like Bryan, I thought he was Bryan. I thought Bryan had returned to me.

The tyrannical thing is how learned, how erudite, how clever addicts become about manipulating others with addictions, the persuasive magic they use on their parents, their friends, on all those who so deeply hope for their recovery. When they deal you hope, you grab it, shoot it, suck it. When your son says, "I'm doing a lot better, Mom. I just need to get through this week. I just need a little money for this week, and next week I'm going to put down . . ." Well, you know what you do. You act like it's true, because, uh-huh, it gives you hope.

When it was frightening to see him, when he weighed only ninety-seven pounds and had turned yellow from jaundice, I believed him when he said he'd been cutting down, he just needed money for a new jacket. "It's November, and it's getting cold, Mom. I need a new jacket. . . ." And I gave him the money for a new jacket. And proved my addiction was worse than his.

The unfaceable thing is your powerlessness. You see the day-by-day decimation of your son, but your role is that of a spectator. You can't stand in the middle of the road and flag down the truck that's carrying him. You can't give him your heart, your innards, the resolve you used to have.

When Morgan said, "Mom, Bryan's dead," I wasn't shocked. I didn't go into shock. It didn't happen. I'll decide when it happens, when I'm ready, if ever. That's the thought my mind produced at the moment. If I had actually heard Morgan's words, taken them inside me, I wouldn't be alive now. I would have started to leak. Blood would have started to leak out of me, and I would have bled to death. I couldn't have accepted it. It couldn't be. . . .

I feel Bryan's presence always. I love him so, and I know how much he loved me, and I know he'd be with me every second if he could, just as when I die, I'm not going to be gone. I'll be with my children. I'll never be away from them.

You can't kill me. I don't believe in life after death and all that. I don't believe I'm going to sit at the right hand of God. When I was six, and they told me God was watching me, I said, "Oh no, you're not watching me. I don't want you watching me, so don't. Watch somebody else."

These are the thoughts that arise when I think about Bryan.

Dancing with the Stars

I realize that when I began to write this autobiography, there was an inner voice, quiet, unintelligible, but very much there, asking, *What are you going to write about? What parts, what aspects of your life? What do you have to say that's really interesting?*

It would have been hard to answer those questions then. But now, having written as much as I have and knowing I'm nearing the end of the book, I'm tapped on the shoulder by some of the things I didn't say that I want to. So I'll discuss those before I tell the tale of *Dancing with the Stars*, how it began, the tumultuous events of each demanding day, the indignation from some that an eighty-two-year-old woman, any eighty-two-year-old woman, should throw herself around in front of a huge TV audience, and the applause from others who thought that an eighty-two-year-old woman, any eighty-two-year-old woman, taking on that challenge was showing some late-in-life guts and what she was doing was something the human race could be proud of—and let me tell you, if

you're twenty-two or eighty-two and you're not a professional dancer, at the very first rehearsal, even more the
first time you dance on the show, you are scared, nervous
too, excited yes, but underneath you are frightened. You
are going to be out on that stage, just you and the professional dancer and you are frightened at the ghastly mis-
steps you might make, at the calamitous fool you could
show yourself to be.

But before I bring the lights up on that little continent
of my life, here first, and in no particular order, are those
memories that were tapping me on the shoulder to be included.

What Do You Call Them? Trysts, Affairs, Dalliances?

I want an honest answer. Does anyone out there who is my age or even twenty or thirty years younger remember every single person he or she had sex with? I am exempting, of course, religious people who have taken the vow of chastity, though on second thought, maybe some of them should be asked the question, too. I like to think I remember every male face that was juxtaposed next to mine. I want to. I hope I do . . . but every once in a while, a smiling, boyish countenance will come from the back of my mind to the front, and I'll have to include him among those I remember.

The odd thing is, sometimes I don't remember whether we actually did the hucklebuck, or whether we just did what in my girlhood was called necking or heavy petting. Necking was kissing and embracing in the front seat—cars all had bench seats in the front—but it involved no touching above the waist. Heavy petting was major rubbing and exploring of the body of the one with whom you were entwined. It stopped short of what we now call penetration, and sometimes the participants would damn near burn out the braking system to keep from crossing that divide.

But I digress. Whatever the actual count is, the list of men with whom I was intimate does not run from here to China. Some featured ones. The dalliances listed below took place when George and I were separated.

Gene Hackman

One spring day, in 1973, as I was walking down Fifth Avenue in New York, I saw coming toward me my old friend, the writer and actor George Furth. With him was Gene Hackman. As we began chatting, George bubbled over with the idea that Gene and I were a perfect match and that we should absolutely "get together." Gene and I were amused at George's enthusiasm, but there was little to take seriously on this sunny afternoon amid New York's pedestrian traffic. We continued our cordial conversation, then went our separate ways.

I'm not sure how long after, probably two or three years, I was in San Francisco, making a film, and in the lobby of my hotel, I ran into Gene. We hadn't seen each other since that moment in New York. We laughed as we recalled it, then decided to honor George's enthusiasm by having dinner together. We met in the hotel dining room. The dinner began casually enough. We truly did enjoy each other's company. Then, as we moved into the main course, it was as if a cosmic wind enveloped us. Some giant space magnet was pulling us together. We didn't finish the meal. We went upstairs, flew into bed, and made love. It was epic. And the next morning, Gene went back to his film, and I went back to mine.

I haven't seen Gene since that night, but I remember well the feisty lad he was.

Peter Viertel

When I was making the 1974 motion picture *Daisy Miller*, after we finished shooting in Rome, the production moved to Vevey, Switzerland. We stayed at the old and lovely Hôtel des Trois Couronnes. This was traditional, many-generations-wealthy Europe. A good number of the residents had lived there for years, and a substantial number of them were in their nineties, so there was tradition and formality all around us.

In the hotel's garden one day, the writer Peter Viertel and I happened to be having lunch at the same time. Peter would later become most well-known for writing the screenplay to the 1990 film *White Hunter Black Heart*, which was based on his novel of the same name and was directed by Clint Eastwood. He saw me and came over to my table. I didn't know Peter terribly well. He was a good friend of Sydney Chaplin's, but he was not as close to George, though he and George frequently played tennis together. He was married to Deborah Kerr then and stayed married to her till she died.

Peter was interesting to me. He was born in Dresden, Germany, and came with his mother, the writer and actress Salka Viertel, to Los Angeles in the early thirties.

Salka Viertel wrote a number of screenplays, especially for her two intimate friends, Greta Garbo and Marlene Dietrich, and she wanted to make films. But Salka became most famous for the gatherings at her home, a perfect English cottage in Santa Monica Canyon, near the beach. That charming place became a salon for many of the industry's elite—director Billy Wilder, Bertolt Brecht, Johnny "Tarzan" Weissmuller, writer Christopher Isherwood, composer Arnold Schoenberg, Norman Mailer, and John Huston.

I knew about Peter's background, and I found Peter attractive, not so much because he awakened a geyser of passion in me, but because of where he'd been, what he'd done, and the people he'd known and been close to. We talked long into the afternoon and then had dinner together. Spending the night together, which we did, was, for me, more something that seemed appropriate, rather than a coupling lit by sexual fire. I remember being amused at Peter's Germanic sense of order. At one point I tousled his hair and pushed it back off his forehead. He promptly pushed it forward again (I think, to cover his bald spot), that was the way it was supposed to be, not any other way.

So my night with Peter Viertel was not so much a dalliance as a cultural excursion. It was interesting but not inflammatory.

Andy Williams

Andy Williams and I had known each other since we were eight years old in Des Moines, when I was studying piano with his aunt, Cornelia Williams Hurlbut. I didn't know it, but Andy had had a crush on me—more than that, a yen for me—ever since those baby days.

In the late seventies, Joan Collins was married to Anthony Newley, she wanted to make peace with me so she invited George and me to their home for dinner one evening. Andy Williams was among the stars present, and on that night he told me of his enduring passion for me. It seemed terribly romantic that ever since his boyhood, I'd been the woman of his dreams.

We chirped and laughed and clucked about it through the evening and decided this story should have a spectacular climax. Two weeks after that dinner, Petula Clark was opening at the Ambassador Hotel. It was going to be a big, glamorous event. George was going to be in Europe, so we decided that on that night we would bring to reality the dream that had so long persisted in Andy's mind. We'd attend Petula Clark's opening, then go off to a palatial hotel suite and begin our tryst with caviar and champagne.

On the appointed night, Andy showed up with an absolutely hideous cold. He was wreckage, leaking and wheezing and blowing his nose nonstop. This condition substantially blurred the glamorous picture we'd created. Nevertheless, we pressed on with the evening. He had planned the rest of it with such care, we had to bring it to its glorious conclusion.

As we left the gala event in Andy's car, still trying to be buoyant and intimate, though his cold symptoms had worsened, he asked me to get his glasses out of the glove compartment. When I opened it, a cascade of photographs fell onto the floor and into my lap. All were handsome shots of his wife and his daughter.

There was not much either of us could say. It was apparent to both of us where Andy's heart lay, and I could see, as I looked through the photographs of these two beautiful women, why what we'd planned wasn't to be and oughtn't to be. Andy took me home, and the evening of revelry we'd planned ended not in a fiery affair but as it should have, with a light, friendly kiss.

Bobby Darin

In 1968 Bobby Darin came to our house on Rockingham to see if he wanted to lease it while our family was in Rome, where George was producing *The Shoes of the Fisherman*. At that time I thought Bobby Darin was kind of silly, because, among other things, I had once passed him on the Sunset Strip while he was driving a flashy convertible, and he had appeared to me to be trying too hard to look cool with his gold jewelry and hip clothes.

During his visit to our house, he met my mother, and they talked openly and avidly. It seemed like the beginning of a love affair. As time passed, my impression of Bobby changed, and I realized he was a genuine, deep, and caring person. We talked about our lives. It was as if we'd known each other for a long time. I cried about some of the things in my life. Bobby urged me to go back to work. We met several times, and one day we had an enchanting afternoon at his house in Malibu.

In 1972 Bobby and I made a film together in Lunenburg, Nova Scotia, titled *Happy Mother's Day, Love George*. Patricia Neal and Ron Howard were also in the cast, and the film was directed by Darren McGavin. Bobby and I had a wonderful time up there in Canada away from the sights and sounds of Los Angeles.

There were the usual minor conflicts that take place in a film company on location. Darren McGavin and Pat Neal were upset because I didn't put my seven-year-old daughter, Dinah, to bed at seven thirty. For me, everything worked fine, and there was no problem with Dinah, so we all carried on with our work and our lives.

Pat's daughter was also in the film, and ultimately, we all became close. Pat had had serious problems in her life. A couple of years ago she'd had three strokes in one week and there was trouble in her marriage so we tried hard to bolster her spirits through the difficult time.

One odd thing I remember about Lunenburg all the restaurants served meals that were totally white—white plates, white potatoes, white cabbage, white napkins, white table cloths, and white fish. We had to bribe the local fishermen to give us something more edible and colorful, because everything they caught was being sent out to market.

As I look back on these trysts or dalliances, something stands out that I hadn't noticed before. All of them had a brief life; some only a single night. I don't know what that says, but there it is.

Dancing with the Stars, Part Two

The minute I wrote those words, two images lit my mind. The first one makes me laugh. I'm with Corky Ballas, my partner, at the end of our "jive" dance. He has my ankles in his hands and is pushing me like a wheelbarrow across the stage. I'm facedown, and my arms, like a lizard's front legs, are keeping the top half of my body off the floor. What I am doing is called "the worm." The audience is rocking with laughter, and now so am I. My arms give out, and I slump to the floor. Corky gallantly picks me up, and we walk toward the judges.

The second image is completely opposite in character: it's frightening. I relive the fright as I write about it. Corky and I are dancing the cha-cha. He's holding my outstretched hand as I twirl toward him. When I get to him, I am supposed to bend forward and extend my right leg behind me and my right arm out in front so my body is parallel to the floor. During rehearsals, Corky said we had to get this preparation right, or the lift and spin that followed could be dangerous. We rehearsed the actual lift and spin only once; it was too scary for me to do it more than that. "I'll be ready to do it on the night of the performance," I assured him. But when the moment arrives to do the lift and spin on the live telecast, I am fearful about it. I can't control my body well, and at the end of my turns toward Corky, I present my left leg instead of my right to him, and my right arm bangs against his forehead. He would need an anatomical chart to figure out where my top and bottom are.

But Corky Ballas has been through every imaginable catastrophe in ballroom dancing, and that night, somehow staying in time with the music, he wrenches the uncontoured mass that is my body around till he has my right arm and my right leg in his hands. He jerks me up and begins to spin. I'm facing death. My teeth nearly hit the floor as he swoops me low, and then I'm sailing four feet above the floor in the parabola he's designed. A death wail escapes me, but it goes unheard due to the howling of the audience members, who don't quite believe what they're seeing. I estimate my centrifugal force to be just under the speed of sound. Fright stiffens every fiber of my body in the eternity before Corky sets me down. The audience roars and cheers. The applause is sustained, and I walk around, taking bows and waving. Then Corky and I head toward the judges.

I was voted off the show that night. One of the judges, Carrie Ann Inaba, said it was painful to have to watch my undeserving performance when Toni Braxton, who is a better dancer, had been voted off the show the week before. There was booing. Many people felt that what she said was cruel and that she had stepped outside her role as judge by expressing her personal feelings. I didn't take to heart what she said; I wasn't offended by it. I thought the score she gave me was probably correct, and I thought she didn't mean any harm.

The next day I flew to New York to be on *The View*, where Corky and I would reprise our dance. Mama mia, we'd be doing that spin again. The show started with a brief chat with the interviewers, and then Corky and I were on center stage. The first part of the dance went smoothly, but I was as rigid as a board when we approached the spin. I don't remember what part of my anatomy I delivered to Corky, but he had to practice even deeper chiropractic techniques to crank my body into the right shape. But again, he would not be denied; he lifted me into the spin. When it was over, I had the feeling I was dead, that I was right next to heaven. I felt I had no brain, no existence. The interviewers saw my state and had a chair brought over for me.

As I look back at these moments and the others that crowd in, I think, how did I get into all this? What karma led me to be on *Dancing with the Stars*? I think, basically, it was my chutzpah. You know what chutzpah is? Unmitigated pushiness. One definition I heard of chutzpah is a girl kills both her parents, then throws herself on the mercy of the court because she's an orphan.

Four years ago I mentioned to my then manager that I wanted to be on *Dancing with the Stars*, DWTS. I don't remember getting a reply, but some months later I heard that DWTS had turned down the idea, saying I was too old.

I also heard DWTS had denied that was the reason. Years later, when my son George became my manager, he said, "Mom, if you could do anything in the world, what would it be?"

I didn't ponder; I didn't muse or meditate. The answer came out easily. "*Dancing with the Stars.*"

"Any particular reason?"

I paused. I hadn't actually thought about why I wanted to be on the show. "Before I die," I said, "I want to experience something extraordinary. Being on *Dancing with the Stars* seems like something extraordinary."

"Okay, let's hook it up," he responded.

I don't know what obstacles, what resistance he and Nevin Dolcefino and Steve LaManna, my agents at Innovative Artists, ran into, but I do know it was not an immediate sell. I'm not sure how, but George and Nevin and Steve convinced the producers of *Dancing with the Stars* that they ought to at least meet with me.

The meeting was held at the ABC offices. Conrad Green, DWTS executive producer, Deena Katz, the producer in charge of talent, and John Saade, Brandon Riegg, and Vicki Dummer of ABC were all waiting for me. During the meeting, for emphasis, I used a number of profane words. As the meeting broke up and we were hugging and saying good-bye, I said, "Wait a minute. I don't want to be the only one who used swear words, so I'm not leaving till everyone else says one."

Everybody did. Except Vicki. She couldn't get a certain word out. She'd get as far as "shh" . . . then couldn't finish. We helped her; we said it with her. "Shit!" we crowed in unison.

The report on the meeting was enthusiastic. The producers asked me to participate in a three-hour rehearsal with one of their dancing staff to see if I could handle the moves. It was serious business: a camera crew videotaped the whole workout. I passed with no problem. Next, I had to list my physical problems: osteoporosis, asthma, 28 percent lung capacity, a bad knee, and high blood pressure.

Dr. Jamie Davis, my chief physician, said he didn't think my knee was strong enough to meet the demands of the show, and he wouldn't sign off on my doing it. So right then, very quickly, the plans for *Dancing with the Stars* were dead. But George persisted; he asked Dr. Davis to get a second opinion. My X-rays were forwarded to an orthopedist, and he said he felt I was good to go if I had a steroid shot. So the knee problem was taken care of.

Then came the blood pressure. The DWTS medical staff said my blood pressure would have to be taken at the beginning of every rehearsal, and it could not be higher than 120/70. More meetings ensued between George and the producers, and the values were revised to 140/80. I took pills twice a day to lower my blood pressure, the first one at 7:00 a.m., because it took five hours for them to kick in, and I had to be ready to rehearse at noon.

There was one other problem I had to deal with, and for me, it was the most difficult obstacle—exhaustion. When I got out of bed in the morning, I was exhausted, and I was exhausted all through the day. That exhaustion bothered me more than any of the medical specifics. I would have to pull myself through rehearsals and make myself stay awake on the way to an interview. On one television show, I was asked what effect *Dancing with the Stars* had had on my career. "It got me out of bed," I said. That sounded flippant, but it wasn't. The demands of the show, what I was called on to do every day, helped me combat my exhaustion.

There were more medical ins and outs, but ultimately, all the issues were settled. With the preliminaries behind me, I turned to the show. I went to my first rehearsal with Corky Ballas. Corky is forty-eight and looks maybe thirty-seven. I found out later what a remarkable life he's had. In the 1980s he was the American ballroom champion five years in a row. Then he moved to England, where ballroom dancing is taken far more seriously and is much more popular than it is here. He became British champion and ultimately world champion. He's also a fine father. His son Mark is an expert ballroom dancer, too. Last year he and his partner won the *Dancing with the Stars* Championship.

For this first rehearsal, we were at a Brazilian martial-arts studio on Ocean Park Boulevard in Los Angeles. That's another thing you don't think about. Every one of the stars and their partners have to have a rehearsal studio for six hours each day. Given the different places we rehearsed, it seemed to me DWTS must have booked every available rehearsal studio in Los Angeles.

The first thing Corky had me do was walk. He stood beside me, and we walked forward, then backward. Then we stepped sideways. He called it the "excuse me" step, because when you go to your seat in a theater, you say "Excuse me, excuse me," as you sidestep over people's feet. Corky watched carefully to see what I could and could not do. He saw that my step was very small, only fourteen inches, and needed to be extended. He had me pull against restraining rubber strips to help me achieve that longer step. He stressed the importance of my weight always being on my standing foot. "You have to push off your standing foot and move into the dance," he would say. Corky explained that there were eight basic moves in any partnering dance, and when you learned those, you could adapt them to any dance.

During the first three weeks, Corky put comedy passages into our choreography, because he didn't think I could actually "dance." After the third week, I, having survived the rigors of the previous two, was in better condition and saw more clearly how serious every week's challenge was, so we focused harder on the dancing. On the fourth show, we did the tango, which I think was my best effort.

Each week, on Tuesday night, on *Dancing with the Stars*, you're given new music for a new dance. Your partner/choreographer begins to sketch out the dance's structure that night, and you have your first rehearsal the next day, Wednesday. On the following Monday night, you have to perform the new dance live in front of twenty million TV viewers. Owing to this rigorous schedule, you're forced into an intimacy. You and your partner are together for extended hours every day, and during every minute of those hours, you have to work physically and at an unrelenting pace. Your partner is a superb dancer, and you know little about the art. He is constantly getting you to bend in ways you never thought possible and to do spins and slides for which you are spectacularly unprepared. Inevitably, fatigue and despair set in; inevitably, you feel fed up with your partner, weary of his constantly asking you to do more. I certainly got weary, I got in Corky's face, and I used profanity.

Corky had, of course, worked with women stars before, but none of them, I think, came within twenty-five years of my age, and probably none had my antagonism toward authority. I think Corky must have studied the analects of Confucius, who taught his followers to be "a wise bamboo." "When the strong wind comes, the wise bamboo bends; it does not break," the master said. Corky never broke, never lost his cool. He always knew how to respond. Sometimes when I loosed a string of profanities, he'd spit out something longer and more colorful and funnier.

I discussed before the outstanding organization that lies behind *Dancing with the Stars*. I didn't see all of it—I couldn't go into every corner—but I'd like to single out one area of activity that's representative of the whole. Each week each dancer and each star gets a new costume. That costume is made from scratch. It is conceived and executed by or under the direction of Randall Christensen, who's been designing these costumes since season two. His work starts the minute the new music is handed out. Along with the sketching and selecting he has to do, he must use diplomacy, a necessary tool. He says stars sometimes have unrealistic ideas about their body types, about what they can and cannot wear, and that's where diplomacy comes in.

The day after every *Dancing* broadcast, Randall races against time to buy fabric and other materials for the following week's costumes, embarking on a rocket-propelled shopping spree. For instance, by the end of the season, one and a half million rhinestones will have been bought. Each costume costs between three and five thousand dollars and is used only once.

I'll always remember Randall's inexhaustible patience when I made a fuss or made a suggestion, and the fun of going upstairs to the costume department to have another fitting and to watch the splendor of his work come to life around me.

My appearance on *Dancing with the Stars* gave me a tsunami of publicity and recognition. I can't go anywhere, literally anywhere, without people greeting me, stopping me, saying how funny I'd been, or telling me how they'd been moved, what they'd learned about life from watching me on the show. I have garnered accolades from people I meet on the street and in restaurants, and I've read some of the e-mails that praise me, that thank me for reminding the sender that at any age, you can do something with your life.

It's all unreal in a way. I feel when I read these things or listen to the compliments from strangers that they're talking about someone else. Because inside, I am still little Cloris, little baby Tortie from Des Moines, small for my age, a head shorter than any other girl. I'm still that little girl who went from carrying water on our little acreage in eastern Des Moines to these glamorous hours.

With my appearance on *Dancing with the Stars*, I entered a wonderful world filled with wonderful people. The several months I was among them was a small lifetime when the world belonged only to us. So now I bid a reluctant goodbye and give a wave of thanks as I turn to my next adventure—being grand marshal of the Rose Parade on New Year's Day.

A Summing Up

I come back to that collision of feelings that had me in thrall at the beginning. It's too late, too late to try to condense what I've experienced into one meerschaum pipe full of wisdom. Wisdom. There's a word. Does anybody know what it means? If somebody said something wise to me right now, would I know it was wise? Part of me says it's too late to think about all that. That other part chimes right in and says it's too early. I'm still a girl, I'm out dancing, and I'd better be home soon so Daddy doesn't get pissed, because I'm out all night.

I'm angry that we have to die. Whoever figured out that part of the process did a really poor job, if you ask me. Why should we have to die? We're born. We get all involved with life, building love affairs and families and businesses and Super Bowl teams, and then, pffft, it's over. You're dead; I'm dead. Death erases all the striving, and all we cared about, worried about, wondered about, were even ready to die for—is gone. Tell me. Is there any goodness in that?

There are two quotes from the French Renaissance

writer Michel Montaigne—George introduced me to him—that have "wisdom" in them, I think. The first is "It isn't the arrival that matters. It's the journey along the way." That's good. We're all on a journey, so concentrate on making it as good, as fun laden as possible, and don't dwell on its end. Here's the other: "The value of your life is not in the number of days you live, but in the use you make of those days. A person may be alive for many years but have lived very little. "

I remember a line from a song that was popular when I was ten years old. "Life is just a bowl of cherries, so live and laugh at it all." That's about as good a piece of philosophy as I can think of. I guess what I feel boils down to a few sentences. Live my life, be with my family, and have a happy face for tomorrow. There could be more Emmys and Oscars ahead—why not?—and if not those, maybe there will be other, less gaudy trophies. There are paths I've not walked before, fields I've yet to roam. So I'm going to get to it; every day I will go out the front door and live my life.

That's it. I don't have any pearls of "wisdom" to leave behind, no letters from Lord Chesterfield to his son, no speech by Polonius to Laertes. But I'd like my children and grandchildren and great-grandson to know this about me: The marrow of me, the person who lives way down inside of me, is a giver of hugs. I'm not sure what started it, but all through my life, I've hugged people. Sometimes, in a restaurant, on the way to my table, I'll stop for a moment and chat with some of the other diners. And before I move on, almost always one of them, a man or a woman, will stand up, and we'll have a hug. And a little message is sent above the crowded voices of our lives, that just for a moment, we did something wonderful. We stopped and gave each other a hug.

Well, you can't put your arms through a book, and it wouldn't be possible to stop at the houses of everyone who's reading this, but I want you to know, you who've stayed to the end of the book, that from way over here, without any dilution of intensity, with all the feeling she has in her, Cloris is putting her arms around you, so that just for a fleeting moment in this journey we're on, we paused and did something wonderful. We hugged each other.